REVISING
PROSE

THIRD EDITION

REVISING
PROSE

Richard A. Lanham

University of California, Los Angeles

Allyn and Bacon
Boston · London · Toronto · Sydney · Tokyo · Singapore

ISBN 0-02-367445-8

Printed in the United States of America

10 9 8 7 6   00 99 98 97 96 95

PREFACE

Revising Prose differs from other writing texts. Let me emphasize these differences up front.

1. About *revising.* True to its title, it is about *revising*; it does not deal with original composition. In colleges and universities, revising is much more common nowadays than it was when this book first appeared. Still, except in composition classes, instructors seldom require it or help students revise on their own. Nothing would improve student writing more than steady, detailed revision, but such revision is difficult to do, especially on your own. The process deserves a book to itself. That's what *Revising Prose* tries to be.

In the workplace to which school leads, revision usually poses more problems than original composition. At work the "student's dilemma," what to write about, hardly exists. The facts are there, the needs press hard, the arguments lie ready to hand, the deadline impends. The first draft assembles itself from the external pressures. Then the sweat really begins — *revision* — commonly done in group settings. For much business writing, collective revision up through a hierarchy determines the final text. "All writing is rewriting," goes the cliché. Okay. Here's the book for it. It offers a collective writing philosophy which a group can easily and quickly learn to share.

2. Translates The Official Style into English. A specific analytical and social premise informs *Revising Prose*: Much bad writing today comes not from the conventional sources of verbal dereliction—sloth, original sin, or native absence of mind—but from stylistic imitation. It is learned, an act of stylistic piety which imitates a single style, the bureaucratic style I have called *The Official Style*. This bureaucratic style dominates written discourse in our time, and beginning or harried or fearful writers adopt it as a protective coloration. So common a writing pattern deserves a separate focus, a book of its own.

3. Rule-based and self-teaching. *Revising Prose* was written to be a supplementary text for any course or task that requires writing. The pressures of school or workplace rarely permit time off to take a special writing course. You need something useful right then. Again, a special book for this purpose seems justified. Because it addresses a single discrete style, *Revising Prose* can be *rule-based* to a degree which prose analysis rarely permits. This set of rules—the *Paramedic Method* (PM)—in turn allows the book, with the aid of its accompanying Exercise Book, to be self-teaching.

4. Useful in all jobs. Because The Official Style dominates university, workplace, and government alike, *Revising Prose* can work in all these contexts. Readers of earlier editions have sometimes asked me whether *Revising Prose* addresses students or teachers. It addresses the revising self in all of us—students, teachers, and all other workers in the world. That revising self is neither the writing self nor the reading self, but a third self which uneasily combines both. Scholars who study children's language have argued that language-understanding and language-using evolve as separate systems which only later combine into full language competence. Revising tries to hold these two different powers, two different selves, in mind at once. That's what makes it so hard. In my experience, the land of revision is an egalitarian place where pedagogical authority gives way to common perplexity. Thus *Revising Prose* addresses an audience including students and teachers but is not restricted to them.

5. Based on the electronic word. If writing on an electronic screen has revolutionized prose composition and prose style, nowhere has the revolution hit harder than in revision. Revision is much easier to do on screen; more of it is being done and done in many new ways. Electronic text brings with it a new stylistic theory as well as a new means of moving words around on an expressive surface. I have tried to infuse the third edition of *Revising Prose* with an awareness of this new writing medium.

6. Saves time and money when used as directed. The bottom line for the workplace: The Paramedic Method, when used as directed, saves time and money. Lots of it. The lard factor of The Official Style usually runs about 50% and eliminating it generates equivalent savings. The bottom line for students: you can say twice as much in the space allotted you, and therefore get a better grade. When an instructor is plowing through a batch of papers at two in the morning, a well-written, powerful train of thought shines out like the Holy Grail. And student time is money, too.

But the book has an even larger efficiency in view—stylistic self-consciousness. This verbal self-awareness, however generated, is like riding a bicycle. Once learned, never forgotten. And stylistic self-consciousness changes how we read and write not only in a single bureaucratic register but across the board. From a particular focus, this book aims to teach a general skill with words, and to suggest that such a skill has moral implications, implications I have dealt with in the last chapter, "Why Bother?"

7. Sentence-based. My last point and the most important. *Revising Prose* focuses on the single sentence. Get the basic architecture of the English sentence straight, I think, and everything else will follow. Transposed up an octave toward generality, this book might have been called *The English Sentence*. We're analyzing in this book the microeconomics of prose. All our work together will be close-focus writing and what acousticians call *near-field listening*. Such close-focus work is as seldom performed as it is universally needed. We spend a great deal of time worrying about our verbal p's and q's that we ought to spend worrying about our sentence architecture. That's where the big misunderstandings occur.

I've called my basic procedure for revision the Paramedic Method because it provides emergency therapy, a first-aid kit, a quick, self-teaching method of revision for people who want to translate The Official Style, their own or someone else's, into plain English. But it is just that—a first-aid kit. It's not the art of medicine. As with paramedicine in underdeveloped countries, it does not attempt to teach a full body of knowledge but only to diagnose and cure the epidemic disease. It won't answer, though at the end it addresses, the big question: having the cure, how do you know when, or if, you should take it? For this you need the full art of prose medicine. (I've addressed this larger stylistic domain in another book, *Analyzing Prose*, which can profitably be read as a sequel to this one.)

The only real cure for America's literacy crisis is a mature and reflective training in verbal self-awareness. Once you have this, you'll see and correct ordinary mistakes almost in passing. If you don't have it, no amount of rule memorization will produce good prose. For prose style, like the rest of human experience, is too various to be adequately described by rules. We don't write by rule but by imitation—as we all realize when we find ourselves producing The Official Style. People often argue that writing cannot be taught, and if they mean that inspiration cannot be commanded nor laziness banished, then of course they are right. But stylistic analysis—revision—is something else, a method, not a mystical rite. How we compose—pray for the muse, marshal our thoughts, find willpower to glue backside to chair—these may be idiosyncratic, but revision belongs to the public domain. Anyone can learn it.

The best introduction to the book *Revising Prose*, especially if you are working in a group, is the half-hour video of the same name, also available from Macmillan. Start by viewing that. The whole book should be presented on an interactive videodisc and perhaps in the future it will be, but until then even a passive videotape shows writing to be a process whose interior dynamics the printed page can but imperfectly express. And perhaps my voice on the tape will animate the print—some readers, at least, have found it so.

To get the most out of *Revising Prose*, use the *Revising Prose Self-Teaching Exercise Book* which accompanies it. Don't cheat and look at the answers; do the revisions first. I've provided exercises for several levels of audience. Do them all. Prose revision is an interactive process *par excellence*, and interaction can occur in a print medium only by filling in the blanks. Do it. And follow the Paramedic Method. It works only if you *follow* it rather than *argue* with it. When it tells you to get rid of the prepositional phrases, get rid of them. Don't go into a "but, well, in this case, given my style, really I need to . . ." bob and weave. You'll never learn anything that way. The Paramedic Method constitutes the center of this book. Use it. It is printed on both the inside front cover of the book and on a separate page in the front. Clip it out and tack it above your desk for easy reference.

I've provided an Appendix which defines the key terms used in the text and an Index which makes using the text as a reference easy.

R. A. L.

For their assistance in the preparation of this edition, I would like to thank the following reviewers: Mary E. Bannon, University of Florida; Sandra Maresh Doe, Metropolitan State College of Denver; William T. Liston, Ball State University; Kenneth L. Risdon, University of Minnesota, Duluth; David Rosenwasser, Muhlenberg College.

In this book, as in all my work, the editorial and scholarly eye of my wife, Carol Dana Lanham, has spared both reader and author many inconsistencies, gaffes, and stupidities. *Gratias Ago.*

CONTENTS

REVISING
PROSE

THE PARAMEDIC METHOD

1. Circle the prepositions.
2. Circle the "is" forms.
3. Ask, "Where's the action?" "Who's kicking who?"
4. Put this "kicking" action in a simple (not compound) active verb.
5. Start fast—no slow windups.
6. Write out each sentence on a blank sheet of paper and mark off its basic rhythmic units with a "/".
7. Read the passage aloud with emphasis and feeling.
8. Mark off sentence lengths in the passage with a "/".

CHAPTER 1

WHERE'S THE ACTION?

Since we all live in a bureaucracy these days, it's not surprising that we end up writing like bureaucrats. Nobody feels comfortable writing simply "Boy meets Girl." The system requires something like "A romantic relationship is ongoing between Boy and Girl." Or "Boy and Girl are currently implementing an interactive romantic relationship." Or still better, "It can easily be seen that an interactive romantic relationship is currently being implemented between Boy and Girl." Contrived examples? Here are some real ones. A businessman denied a loan does not suffer but instead says that "I went through a suffering process." A teacher does not say, "If you use a calculator in class, you will never learn to add and subtract," but instead, "The fact is that the use of the calculator in the classroom is negative for the learning process." An undergraduate wants to say, "Lungsick Inc. and other companies have spent years trying to find a substitute for asbestos." But it comes out, "Identification of an acceptable substitute for asbestos in asphalt mastics has been the subject of research by Lungsick Inc. and other manufacturers for several years." A politician "indicates his reluctance to accept the terms on which the proposal was offered" when he might have said "No." A teacher of business writing tells us not that "People entering business today must learn to speak effectively," but "One of these factors is the seemingly increasing awareness of the idea that to succeed in business, it is imperative that the young person entering a business career possess definite skill in oral communication."

The Official Style comes in many dialects—government, military, social scientific, lab scientific, MBA flapdoodle—but all exhibit the same basic attributes. They all build on the same central imbalance, a dominance of nouns and an atrophy of verbs. They enshrine the triumph, worshipped in every bureaucracy, of stasis over action. This basic imbalance is easy to cure, if you want to cure it—and this book's Paramedic Method tells you how to do it. But when do you want to cure it? We all sometimes feel, whatever setting we write in, that we will be penalized for writing in plain English. It will sound too flip. Unserious. Even satirical. In my academic dialect, that of literary study, writing plain English nowadays is tantamount to walking down the hall naked as a jaybird. Public places demand protective coloration; sometimes you must write in The Official Style. And when you do, how do you make sure you are writing a good kind of Official Style—if there is one—rather than a bad one? What can "good" and "bad" mean when applied to prose in this way?

Revising Prose starts out by teaching you how to revise The Official Style. But after you've learned that, we'll reflect on what such revision is likely to do for, or to, you in the bureaucratic world of the future—and the future is only going to get more bureaucratic. You ought then to be able to see what "good" and "bad" mean for prose, and what you are really doing when you revise it. And that means you will know how to socialize your revisory talents, how to put them, like your sentences, into action.

PREPOSITIONAL-PHRASE STRINGS

We can begin with three examples of student prose:

> This sentence is in need of an active verb.

> Physical satisfaction is the most obvious of the consequences of premarital sex.

> In strict contrast to Watson's ability to control his mental stability through this type of internal gesture, is Rosalind Franklin's inability to even conceive of such "playing."

What do these examples have in common? They have been assembled from strings of prepositional phrases glued together by that all-purpose epoxy "is." In each case the sentence's verbal force has been shunted into a noun, and its verbal force has been diluted into "is," the neutral copulative, the weakest verb in the language. Such sentences project no life, no vigor. They just "are." And the "is" generates those strings of prepositional phrases fore and aft. It's so easy to fix. Look for the real action. Ask yourself, who's kicking who? (Yes, I know, it should be *whom*, but doesn't *whom* sound stilted?)

In "This sentence is in need of an active verb," the action obviously lies in "need." And so, "This sentence needs an active verb." The needless prepositional phrase "in need of" simply disappears once we see who's kicking who. The sentence, animated by a real verb, comes alive, and in six words instead of nine.

Where's the action in "physical satisfaction is the most obvious of the consequences of premarital sex"? Buried down there in "satisfaction." But just asking the question reveals other problems. Satisfaction isn't really a consequence of premarital sex, in the same way that, say, pregnancy is. And, as generations of both sexes will attest, sex, premarital or otherwise, does not always satisfy. Beyond all this, the contrast between the clinical phrasing of the sentence, with its lifeless "is" verb, and the life-giving power of lust in action makes

3

the sentence seem almost funny. Excavating the action from "satisfaction" yields "Premarital sex satisfies! Obviously!" This gives us a lard factor of 66% and a comedy factor even higher. (You find the lard factor by dividing the difference between the number of words in the original and the revision by the number of words in the original. In this case, $12 - 4 = 8$; $8 \div 12 = .66$. If you've not paid attention to your own writing before, think of a lard factor (LF) of one-third to one-half as normal and don't stop revising until you've removed it. The comedy factor in prose revision, though often equally great, does not lend itself to numerical calculation.)

But how else do we revise here? "Premarital sex is fun, obviously" seems a little better, but we remain in thrall to "is." And the frequent falsity of the observation stands out yet more. Revision has exposed the empty thinking. The writer makes it even worse by continuing, "Some degree of physical satisfaction is present in almost all coitus." Add it all together and we get something like, "People usually enjoy premarital sex" (LF 79%). At its worst, academic prose makes us laugh by describing ordinary reality in extraordinary language.

The writer discussing James Watson's *The Double Helix* sleepwalks into the standard form of absent-minded academic prose: a string of prepositional phrases and infinitives, then a lame "to be" verb, then more prepositional phrases and infinitives. Look at the structure:

In strict contrast
to Watson's ability
to control his mental stability
through this type
of internal gesture,
is Rosalind Franklin's inability
to even conceive
of such "playing."

Notice how long this laundry list takes to get going? The root action skulks down there in "ability to control." So we revise:

> Watson controls himself through these internal gestures; Rosalind
> Franklin does not even know such gestures exist.

I've removed "in strict contrast" because the rephrasing clearly
implies it; given the sentence two simple root verbs — "controls" and "knows"; and, to make the contrast tighter and
easier to see, used the same word — "gestures" — for the same
concept in both phrases. We've reduced seven prepositional
phrases and infinitives to one prepositional phrase, and thus
banished that DA-da-da, DA-da-da monotony of the original.
A lard factor of 41% but, more important, we've given the
sentence *shape*, and some life flows from its verbs.

The drill for this problem stands clear. Circle every form
of "to be" ("is," "was," "will be," "seems to be," "have been")
and every prepositional phrase. Then find out who's kicking
who and start rebuilding the sentence with that action. Two
prepositional phrases in a row turn on the warning light, three
make a problem, and four invite disaster. With a little practice,
sentences like "The mood Dickens paints is a bleak one" will
turn into "Dickens paints a bleak mood" (LF 35%) almost
before you've written them.

Undergraduates have no monopoly on that central element
in The Official Style, the string of prepositional phrases. Look
at these strings from a lawyer, a scientist, and a critic:

> Here is an example *of* the use *of* the rule *of* justice *in* argumentation.

> One *of* the most important results *of* the presentation *of* the data
> is the alteration *of* the status *of* the elements *of* the discourse.

> *In* the light *of* the association *in* the last quarter *of* the sixteenth
> century *of* wit *with* the means *of* amplification, which consist
> mainly *of* the processes *of* dialectical investigation, this definition
> probably has more validity than has generally been accorded it.

The *of* strings are the worst of all. They seem to reenact
a series of hiccups. When you try to revise them, you can feel

how fatally easy the "is" plus prepositional-phrase Official Style formula is for prose style. They blur the central action of the sentence—you can't find out what is really going on. Let's try revising.

Here is an example *of* the use *of* the rule *of* justice *in* argumentation.

"Rule of justice" is a term of art, so we must leave it intact. After we have found an active verb—"exemplify"—buried in "is an example of the use of," the rest follows easily.

This passage exemplifies argumentation using the rule of justice.

Now, how about the second sentence. It represents a perfect Official Style pattern: string of prepositional phrases + "is" + string of prepositional phrases. Let's diagram it for emphasis:

One

of the most important results
of the presentation
of the data

is the alteration

of the status
of the elements
of the discourse.

See the formulaic character? The monotonous rhythm? The blurred action? I'm not sure what this sentence means, but the action must be buried in "alteration." Start there, with an active, transitive verb—"alter." How about "Presentation of the data alters the status of the discourse elements"? Or less formally, "The status of the discourse elements depends on how you present the data." Or it may mean, "You don't know the status of the elements until you have presented the data." At least two different meanings swim beneath the formulaic prose. To revise it you must *rethink* it.

Now, the third sentence:

> *In* the light
> *of* the association
> *in* the last quarter
> *of* the sixteenth century
> *of* wit
> *with* the means
> *of* amplification,
>   which consist mainly
> *of* the processes
> *of* dialectical investigation,
>   this definition probably has more validity than has generally been accorded it.

Here, the prepositional phrases have been assembled into a gigantic preparatory fanfare for a central action which does not come until the end —

> this definition probably has more validity.

These slow-motion openings, a sure sign of The Official Style, drain all the life from the sentence before we ever get to the verb, and hence the action. I'll revise to get off to a faster start, using my knowledge of what the writer—behind the infarcted prose—was trying to say:

> This definition holds true more than people think, especially considering what wit meant around 1600. (15 words instead of 42; LF 64%)

"BLAH BLAH *IS THAT*" OPENINGS

The formulaic slo-mo opening often provides your first taste of The Official Style. And it is a fatally easy habit to fall into. Let's look at some typical examples of what we will call the "Blah blah *is that*" opening from students, professors, and writers at large:

What I would like to signal here *is that* . . .

My contention *is that* . . .

What I want to make clear *is that* . . .

What has surprised me the most *is that* . . .

The upshot of what Heidegger says here *is that* . . .

The first *is that* . . .

The point I wish to make *is that* . . .

What I have argued here *is that* . . .

My opinion *is that* on this point we have only two options . . .

My point *is that* the question of the discourse of the human sciences . . .

The fact of the matter *is that* the material of this article is drawn directly from . . .

The one thing that Belinda does not realize *is that* Dorimant knows exactly how to press her buttons.

Easy to fix this pattern; just amputate the mindless preludial fanfare. Start the sentence with whatever follows "Blah blah *is that*. . . ." On a word processor it couldn't be simpler: do a global search for the phrase "is that" and revise it out each time. For example:

The upshot of what **Heidegger says** here is that . . .

My opinion is that on this point **we have only two options** . . .

My point is that the question of **the discourse of the human sciences** . . .

The fact of the matter is that **the material of this article is drawn directly from** . . .

We can even improve my favorite from this anthology:

The one thing that **Belinda does not realize** is **that Dorimant knows exactly how to press her buttons.**

By amputating the fanfare, you *start fast*, and a fast start may lead to major motion. That's what we're after. Where's the *action*?

Writers addicted to the "blah blah *is that*" dead rocket often tie themselves in knots with it. One writes: "The position we **are at is this.**" Another: "The traditional opposite notion to **this is that there are.** . . ." And a third, a university professor, in an article accurately titled "On the Weakness of Language in the Human Sciences," offers this spasmodic set of **thises, thats** and **whats**:

Now **what** I would like to know specifically **is this: what is** the meaning of **this** "as" that Heidegger emphasizes so strongly when he says **that "that** which is explicitly understood"—**that is, that** which is interpreted—"has the structure of something as something"? My opinion **is that** what Heidegger means **is that** the structure of interpretation (*Auslegung*) is figural rather than, say, intentional. (Emphasis mine.)

In escaping from this Houdini straitjacket, a couple of mechanical tricks come in handy. Besides eliminating the "is's" and changing every passive voice ("is defended by") to an active voice ("defends"), you can squeeze the compound verbs hard, make every "are able to" into a "can," every "seems to succeed in creating" into "creates," every "cognize the fact that" (no, I didn't make it up) into "think," every "am hopeful that" into "hope," every "provides us with an example of" into "exemplifies," every "seeks to reveal" into "shows," and every "there is the inclusion of" into "includes." Then, after amputating those mindless *fact that* introductory-phrase fanfares, you'll start fast. After that fast start, "cut to the chase," as they say in the movies, as soon as you can. Instead of "the answer is in the negative," you'll find yourself saying "No."

THE PARAMEDIC METHOD

We now have the beginnings of the Paramedic Method (PM):

1. Circle the prepositions.
2. Circle the "is" forms.
3. Ask, "Where's the action?" "Who's kicking who?"
4. Put this "kicking" action in a simple (not compound) active verb.
5. Start fast—no slow windups.

Let's use the PM on a more complex instance of blurred action, the opening sentences of an undergraduate psych paper:

The history of Western psychological thought has long been dominated by philosophical considerations as to the nature of man. These notions have dictated corresponding considerations of the nature of the child within society, the practices by which children were to be raised, and the purposes of studying the child.

Two actions here—"dominate" and "dictate"—but neither has fully escaped from its native stone. The prepositional-phrase and infinitive strings just drag them down.

The history
of Western psychological thought . . .
by philosophical considerations
as to the nature
of man.
. . .
of the nature
of the child
within society . . .
by which children . . .
to be raised . . .
of studying . . .

In asking, "Where's the action?" "Who's kicking who?" we next notice all the actions fermenting in the nouns: *thinking* in "thought," *consider* in "considerations," more *thinking* somewhere in "notions." They hint at actions they don't supply and thus blur the actor-action relationship still further. We want, remember, a plain active verb, no prepositional-phrase strings, and a natural actor firmly in charge.

The **actor** must be: "philosophical considerations as to the nature of man."

The **verb:** "dominates."

The **object** of the action: "the history of Western psychological thought."

Now the real problems emerge. What does "philosophical considerations as to the nature of man" really mean? Buried down there is a question: "What is the nature of man?" The "philosophical considerations" just blur this question rather than narrow it. Likewise, the object of the action—"the history of Western psychological thought"—can be simply "Western psychological thought." Shall we put all this together in the passive form that the writer used?

Western psychological thought has been dominated by a single question: What is the nature of man?

Or, with an active verb:

A single question has dominated Western psychological thought: What is the nature of man?

Our formulaic concern with the stylistic surface — passives, prepositional phrases, kicker and kickee — has led here to a much more focused thought.

The first sentence passes its baton very awkwardly to the second. "Considerations," confusing enough as we have seen, become "these notions" at the beginning of the second sentence, and these "notions," synonymous with "considerations" in the first sentence, dictate more but different "considerations" in the second. We founder in these vague and vaguely synonymous abstractions. Our unforgiving eye for prepositional phrases then registers "*of* the nature *of* the child *within* society." We don't need "within society"; where else will psychology study children? And "the nature of the child" telescopes to "the child." We metamorphose "the practices by which children were to be raised" into "child rearing," and "the purposes in studying the child" leads us back to "corresponding considerations of the nature of the child within society," which it seems partly to overlap. But we have now a definite actor, remember, in the first sentence — the "single question." So a tentative revision:

This basic question leads to three others: What are children like? How should they be raised? Why should we study them?

Other revisions suggest themselves. Work out a couple. In mine, I've used "question" as the baton passed between the two sentences because it clarifies the relationship between the two. And I've tried to expose what real, clear action lay hidden beneath the conceptual cotton wool of "these notions have dictated corresponding considerations."

A single question has dominated Western psychological thought: What is the nature of man? This basic question leads to three others. What are children like? How should they be raised? Why should we study them?

This two-sentence example of student academic prose rewards some reflection. First, the sentences boast no grammatical or syntactical mistakes. Second, they need not have come from a student. Any issue of a psychology journal or text will net you a dozen from the same mold. How else did the student learn to write them? Third, not many instructors reading this prose will think anything is wrong with it. Just the opposite. It reads just right; it sounds *professional*. The teacher's comment on this paper reads, in full: "An excellent paper—well conceived, well organized, and well written—A+." Yet a typical specimen sentence from it makes clear neither its main actor nor action; its thought consistently puffs into vague general concepts like "considerations," "notions," and the like; and its cradle-rocking monotonous rhythm puts us to sleep. It reveals a mind writing in formulas, out of focus, above all a mind putting no pressure on itself. The writer is not thinking so much as, on a scale slightly larger than normal, filling in the blanks. You can't build bridges thinking in this muddled way; they will fall down. If you bemuse yourself thus in a chemistry lab, you'll blow up the apparatus. And yet the student, obviously very bright, has been invited to write this way and rewarded for it. He or she has been doing *a stylistic imitation*, and has brought if off successfully. Chances are that the focused, plain-language version I've offered would get a lower grade than the Official Style original. Revision is always perilous and paradoxical, but nowhere more so than in the academic world. Not so perilous, though, as bridges that fall down or lab apparatus that blows up. In the long run, it is better to get your thinking straight and take your chances.

CHAPTER 2

SENTENCE SHAPES AND SHOPPING BAGS

The Official Style, then, builds its sentences on a form of the verb "to be" plus strings of prepositional phrases fore and aft; it buries the action of its verbs in nominative constructions with the passive voice; it often separates the natural subject from the natural verb, actor from action, by big chunks of verbal sludge; it cherishes the long windup and the slo-mo opening. Add all these attributes together and you build a sentence which has no natural shape or rhythm, no structure to express its meaning. Instead, you get something like a shopping bag that the writer stuffs with words, using the generative formulas we have just chronicled. This shapelessness makes them unreadable; read one of them aloud with gusto and emphasis and you'll give yourself the giggles. Try it:

> One of the factors that limits and warps the development of a theory of composition and style by teachers of the subject is the tendency to start with failed or inadequate writing and to project goodness as the opposite of badness.

You feel silly reading this aloud. This typical Official Style sentence has no shape which the voice can use to underline the sense. Nothing in the sentence tells you who the natural subject is—writing teachers—or what that subject is *doing*, where the *action* is. Possible subjects there are aplenty:

    factors
    development
    theory
    composition
    style
    teachers
    subject

And incipient actions too:

    limiting
    warping
    developing
    tending
    starting
    failing
    projecting

But nothing in the sentence's shape narrows down our choice among them. Instead, two almost equal elements glued together by "is":

> One of the **FACTORS** that limits and warps the development of a theory of composition and style by teachers of the subject

> **IS**

> the **TENDENCY** to start with failed or inadequate writing and to project goodness as the opposite of badness.

And notice how far it is from the subject to the verb? Whatever strength their union might have produced evaporates in the space between. (It wasn't much to begin with—"factors" being impossibly general and "is" generically flabby.) And if you break down each part, it falls into equal parts as well:

One of the factors
that limits and warps
the development of a theory
of composition and style
by teachers of the subject

the tendency to start with failed or inadequate writing
and to project goodness as the opposite of badness.

Reading prose aloud—not speed mumbling it but reading it with an actor's care—can tell you a lot about sentence shape. So can another simple technique. Take your sentence and write it by itself on a card or sheet of paper. Try to sketch its architecture, to chart its lines of force. Try even to draw abstract shapes that reflect its meaning. Just look at its shape. If you are working on a word processing program that permits it, box the selection to further frame your attention. On an electronic screen, white space is free. Put your sentence by itself on the screen. Then apply the Paramedic Method to yield a shape which reflects meaning. For our present shape-less sentence, we might isolate the natural subject, "writing teachers," and the natural verb, "tend to start with," and see where they lead.

Writing teachers tend to start with bad writing and to project
good writing as its opposite.

Here at least we have a parallel structure that reflects a parallel meaning:

start with bad writing
project good writing

Subordinate this first point to the second and we get:

> Because writing teachers start with bad writing, and project good writing only as its opposite, they have trouble developing a theory of style.

Or diagrammed:

> <u>Because</u> writing teachers
> start with bad writing,
> and project good writing as its opposite,
> <u>they have trouble</u> **developing a theory of style.**

The parallel elements of good and bad writing are now framed by a causal relationship (underlined elements). The second clause now creates a concluding emphasis, gives the voice and the eye a climax to dwell upon. Try practicing revisions like this on sentences in the *Exercise Book*. (Numbers 5, 8, 9, 12, pp. 3ff. would be a good place to begin.) See if you can get from here:

> Sometimes they were the result of the initiative of male leaders, sometimes of the coming together of women in the same street or workplace.

To here:

Sometimes men led in the same street, sometimes women.

Here the parallelism frames a central assertion from which both elements draw power.

Or work backward. Start with this example of parallel constructions and revise back into The Official Style version:

> People get sick; doctors are needed. Laws are broken; lawyers are needed. Merchandise is sold; businessmen are needed.

People get <u>sick</u>; doctors **are needed.**
Laws are <u>broken</u>; lawyers **are needed.**
Merchandise is <u>sold</u>; businessmen **are needed.**

I've illuminated this sentence to show how many internal relationships—how many suggested meanings—a sentence can
project when it has a meaningful shape. A shaped sentence is
read with reinforcement from the visual cortex of the brain.
You reorganize the sentence in your mind's eye to make con-
nections: People, Laws, Merchandise are being compared;
doctors, lawyers, and businessmen are too, and connected
with the other units of three; the subjects (<u>people, laws, mer-
chandise</u>) are aligned with what is happening to them (<u>sick,
broken, sold</u>). And because each sentence has the same ending
("**are needed**"), the eye wants to diagram the group as I have
done. An expressive pattern—a natural, expressive shape—
lurks beneath even the worst Official Style shopping bag.
Revision's task is to drag it forth and spruce it up.

People who write about language, the earlier example to
the contrary notwithstanding, can write well. Here's another
example, for contrast: "The author will throw a noun or two
at you, wait for your reaction, then throw a few more at you."
Perfect. A believable voice, a nice A-B-A shape. Nothing
needed here except applause.

Often the shopping-bag sentence will begin with a dead-
rocket opening that stuffs everything in before the main verb
and thus finds its action only when about to expire:

The manner in which behavior first shown in a conflict situation
may become fixed so that it persists after the conflict has passed
is then discussed.

The manner (**monstrous filling**) is discussed.

No actor is given by "is discussed," so we'll invent one, our
old English professor, Dormitive H. Guffbag. "Prof. Guffbag

then discusses how behavior which first emerges in conflict persists after the conflict has passed." First the actor, then the action, then two balanced and parallel elements:

> Prof. Guffbag then discusses
>   how behavior which first emerges in conflict
>   persists after the conflict has passed.

The balance and parallel in "emerges–conflict" and "persists–conflict" glue the two elements together. The sentence begins fast, then leads us to a garden whose simple design we can easily comprehend. And the Lard Factor, even after we've added Guffbag-the-actor: 17 instead of 26; LF 35%. Not too shabby. (As a reminder, you compute the Lard Factor by dividing the difference between the number of words in the original and the revision by the number of words in the original. Computing the LF is easy now: most word processors have word-count features and built-in calculators.)

A Jumbo Shopping Bag

Here is a jumbo shopping bag **is** string from a famous historian:

> There **is** one last point in the evidence of Everard of Ypres which deserves a comment before we leave it. This **is** the very surprising difference between the number of students at Gilbert's lectures in Chartres and in Paris. The small number in Chartres **is** perhaps not surprising, for Gilbert **was** a notoriously difficult lecturer; but the very large number in Paris **is** very surprising. Of course, it **is** possible to give several different explanations of these figures, but since the authority for both numbers **is** the same and there **was** no obvious reason for distortion, they should, at least provisionally, be treated seriously.

The absolute formula: strings of prepositional phrases glued together by "is":

There **is** one last point
in the evidence
of Everard
of Ypres which deserves a comment before we leave it.
This **is** the very surprising difference
between the number
of students
at Gilbert's lectures
in Chartres and
in Paris.

No need to continue this charting; you get the idea. The writer, like a daydreaming bagger at the grocery, stuffs his sentence with first one prepositional phrase and then another. Revision? I'll try revising the first two sentences into one:

One last question apropos Everard of Ypres: why did so few students attend his Chartres lectures and so many those in Paris? (LF 44%; 2 prepositions instead of 7).

A POLISH SAUSAGE

Now a monster—a Polish sausage of a sentence—by a well-known sociologist. Any student studying the social sciences will have to read acres of such prose:

The fact that all selves are constituted by or in terms of the social process, and are individual reflections of it—or rather of this organized behavior pattern which it exhibits, and which they comprehend in their respective structures—**is** not in the least incompatible with or destructive of the fact that every individual self has its own peculiar individuality, its unique pattern; because each individual within that process, while it reflects in its organized structure the behavior patterns of that process as a whole, does so from its own particular and unique standpoint within that process, and thus reflects in its organized structure a different aspect or perspective of this whole social behavior pattern from that which is reflected in the organized structure of any other individual self within that process (just as every monad in the Leibnizian universe mirrors that universe from a different point of view, and thus mirrors a different aspect or perspective of that universe).

No definition of a sentence really defines much, but every sentence ought somehow to organize a pattern of thought, even if it does not always reduce that thought to bite-sized pieces. This shapeless hippo, however, has at heart only our getting lost. Notice how far it is from the first subject ("the fact that") to its verb ("is")? We forget the subject before we get to the verb. To bring some shape to this jumbo bag, we'll need, for a start, a full stop after "pattern." "The fact that" translates, as always, into "that." And then we return to changing passive voice to active voice ("are constituted by" to "constitutes"), to eliminating prepositional phrases, to finding out where the action is (Who is kicking who?). And we must attack, too, the compulsive pattern of needless overspecification ("incompatible with or destructive of"), the endemic curse of academic writing from the cradle to the grave. So: "That society (= "the social process") constitutes all selves and they reflect it. . . ."
So far so good. What of the two lines between dashes?

—or rather of this organized behavior pattern which it exhibits, and which they comprehend in their respective structures—

They simply restate, in new gobbledygook terminology, what has preceded. Shred them. And "is not in the least incompatible with or destructive of the fact that" translates into English as "does not in the least destroy." "Every individual self has its own peculiar individuality, its own unique pattern" = "the unique self." We have thus translated the first half of this shopping bag back into English as

That society constitutes all selves and they reflect it, does not in the least destroy the unique self. (18 words instead of 65; LF 72%)

To finish shaping this sentence, we need only add a comma after "selves." Now read it aloud. Subject ("That society constitutes all selves") separated from its verb by only a short parenthetical addition ("and they reflect it") stays in our minds until we reach a direct object ("the unique self"), which falls into the naturally emphatic closing position. The voice ought to rise in pitch for the parenthetic "they reflect" and for "least" and "unique." The sentence shape underscores its meaning rather than burying it. The syntax permits, encourages, the voice to help. The prose has become readable. See if you can clean up the rest of the passage in the same way.

NATURAL SHAPES AND BIG MISTAKES

Looking for the natural shape of a sentence often suggests the quickest way to revision. Consider this example:

> I think that all I can usefully say on this point is that in the normal course of their professional activities social anthropologists are usually concerned with the third of these alternatives, while the other two levels are treated as raw data for analysis.

The action starts with "are usually concerned with." Beginning to build a shape means starting here. "Usually, social anthropologists concentrate on the third alternative." And now, do we really need the whole endless dead-rocket opening, from "I think" to "activities"?

> I think that all I can usefully say on this point is that in the normal course of their professional activities . . .

"In the normal course of their professional activities" = "usually," and the rest is guff. So: "Usually, social anthropologists concentrate on the third alternative and treat the other two as raw data" ("for analysis" being implied by "raw data"). A final polishing moves "usually" to the other side of "social anthropologists" so as to modify "concentrate" more immediately. The sentence then begins strongly, subject–short modifier–verb, and offers two other emphasis points, "third alternative" and "raw data." And shouldn't we subordinate the "treat" by turning it into a participle? The final revision would then read:

> Social anthropologists usually concentrate on the third alternative, treating the other two as raw data.

Read it aloud now and then go back to the original and compare (15 words instead of 45; LF 66%).

Confused. Confusing. Two-thirds longer than it should be. What would a mistake of this magnitude look like in another area of human endeavor? A builder who needs 3 yards of concrete and orders 9? A physician who mistakes the drug and triples the dose? *Big* mistakes. American college students are asked to read a steady diet of this prose—often nothing but. Two lessons, at least, are taught by it: first, often a reader can't understand the assignment, at least not *really*, so just skims it; second, readers, therefore, *need not really pay attention to the words*. Words on a page do not *mean things explicitly*. They only point to generalized meanings in vague formulas.

And so a student writes:

> The most important thing to remember is the fact that interest in the arts has not declined in popularity. (19 words)

instead of

> Interest in the arts has not declined. (7 words; LF 63%)

Or

> The generation of television is a feeble one, it is a generation
> lacking in many areas, especially that of artistic background and
> interest. (23 words)

Here, of course, we don't know whether it is television that
is being generated, or an age group being generated by it. And
who knows what "artistic background and interest" means, or
what the "many areas" might be. So revision becomes both a
guess and a satire:

> The TV generation has shown little interest in art—or in any-
> thing else either. (14 words; LF 39%)

Such a sentence shows not bad writing so much as a listless
imitation of the vague, approximative prose common in Official
Style writing of all sorts. The imitation often becomes exactly
formulaic, as in this nursing-home ad copy:

> Heartfelt House has earned a reputation *for* excellence *for* the
> sharing *of* the wisdom *of* the path *of* compassionate service *in* the
> natural healing arts.

Easy to see the string of prepositional phrases, but you must
ponder the sentence to see the damage done to what might
otherwise have been a thought. What is Heartfelt House good
at? Excellence? Sharing? Wisdom? Path? Compassionate service? Healing arts? It all seems to add up to

> Heartfelt House has a good reputation as a nursing home. (LF
> 60%)

What about this sentence?

> Throughout our lives, we are exposed to a lot of different teach-
> ings and one of them, in our society, is the value placed upon
> a life in which we are successful.

25

Easy to revise:

> Our society teaches the value of success. (LF 77%)

The rest is just floor shavings, left after the thought has been turned on the lathe. But The Official Style always *includes* the floor shavings, feels undressed without them, and so this prose does too. When you cherish the floor shavings of thought, you spell out the obvious: "The UCLA Premed Handbook states that a principal premed question is whether or not to become a physician." Even to say that writing contains needless clichés becomes "Both articles contain several words and phrases that, because of their ambiguous or cliché property, could easily be omitted."

This kind of prose does not come naturally. You have to learn it. And with it comes a habit of reading. Or, rather, this kind of prose asks to be read in a certain way—quickly, inattentively, just for the general drift, the fugitive generalization highlighted—that invites you to write prose of the same kind. Shopping-bag sentences display more than shapeless verbal jumbles, maddening verbosity, and the floor shavings of aborted thoughts. A whole way of reading and thinking stands revealed: vague, unfocused, built on temporary generalities themselves built on hopelessly cluttered heaps of general terms, often ending in Latinate *-ion* "shun" words. When a philosophy student writes

> In the sixth *Meditation* Descartes comes to the conclusion that the mind is distinct from the body.

instead of

> In the sixth *Meditation* Descartes distinguishes the mind from the body.

he or she stands more than a circumlocution away from the tenor and timbre of Descartes's thought. A whole style—The

Official Style—away. And The Official Style has become today, more often than not, the Academic Style.

THE PM VS. A LUMP OF PEANUT-BUTTER PROSE

The Paramedic Method focuses attention on The Official Style's distortions by using simple diagnostic questions. Let's review it, as developed to date.

1. Circle the prepositions.
2. Circle the "is" forms.
3. Ask, "Where's the action?" "Who's kicking who?"
4. Put this action in a simple (not compound) active verb.
5. Start fast—no slow windups.

Now we'll put the PM to work on a paragraph that considers the subject itself—prose.

A piece of prose may be considered sincere if, in some manner, it establishes its credibility to its audience. The degree of sincerity, however, is relative to the type of person reading it. A logical, scientific person would feel gratified if the author included the relationship of counterpoints to his message. To them this technique shows that the author considered opposing viewpoints while presenting his own; an analytical ideal for such an audience. (73 words)

A typical piece of shapeless prose. Tedious. Lifeless. Just plain boring to read. The first sentence ought by its shape to underline the basic contrast of "sincere" with "credible." How about, "Prose will seem sincere if it seems credible"? The parallelism of "seems sincere" and "seems credible" works because the two parallel elements stand close together. Sparks can fly between them. The sentence gains some snap, a shape

(8 words instead of 19; LF 58%). Now for the second sentence. It qualifies the first and should do so obviously. We need an adversative, "but": "But how sincere will depend on the type of reader." Or maybe just "on the reader," "type of" and "kind of" being usually expendable qualifiers. (How expendable you can discover by doing a global search and delete and then reading over what you have written. Notice anything missing?) Now read the last two sentences aloud, and with feeling—*con amore*. Can't be done. Where, though, does your voice *want* to rise, what does it *want* to stress? Obviously "a logical scientific person" and "opposing viewpoints." What shape will model this?

A logical, scientific person = A scientist

would feel gratified = would welcome

if the other included the relationship of counterpoints to his message = would welcome a statement of alternative views.

In the last sentence, "to them" refers back, impossibly enough, to a singular antecedent ("scientific person") and the rest is inane repetition. What follows after the semicolon represents *dieselizing*—the prose engine continuing to run after the key has been turned off. A sense of shape means a feeling for strong closings as well as strong openings. As a revision, then:

A scientist would welcome a statement of alternative views. (9 words for 40; LF 78%)

And for the whole passage:

Prose will seem sincere if it seems credible. But how sincere will depend on the (type of) reader. A scientist would welcome a statement of alternative views.

We've solved a number of problems but we've created some too, first in the sequence of thought and, no less obviously, in the rhythmic interrelation of the three sentences. The prose sounds choppy. Choppiness often emerges in elephantiasis surgery like this. Don't worry. Concentrate on the shape of each sentence. If, as here, you end up with a string of sentences all the same length, this can be fixed later.

To articulate the sequence of thought, we need to join the first two sentences and acknowledge the third as an example:

> Prose will seem sincere if it seems cred . . .

Now the real problem emerges. What depends *directly* on the reader is credibility, not sincerity. The writer was trying to say, "Prose will seem sincere if it seems credible, but how credible will depend on who reads it." "Who reads it" finally gets around the awkward "type of" problem and leads directly to "A scientist." Now that we've gotten this straight, the last sentence follows naturally, to exemplify how credibility varies with the reader: "A scientist, for example, would welcome a statement of alternative views." And so again, the original and the revision:

Original

A piece of prose may be considered sincere if, in some manner, it establishes its credibility to its audience. The degree of sincerity, however, is relative to the type of person reading it. A logical, scientific person would feel gratified if the author included the relationship of counterpoints to his message. To them this technique shows that the author considered opposing viewpoints while presenting his own; an analytical ideal for such an audience. (73 words)

Revision

Prose will seem sincere if it seems credible, but how credible will depend on who reads it. A scientist, for example, would welcome a candid statement of alternative views. (29 words; LF 60%)

I've inserted "candid" both because it clarifies the credibility issue we've just brought into focus, and because the rhythm needs another beat or two here, an adjectival rest before the stressed "statement of alternative views." This back pressure of rhythm on sense illustrates in little just what the whole passage does in large; thought and style feed back on one another continually as you revise prose. Leaning on rhythm means leaning on thought, and vice versa. And the process never ends. When you revise for shape and rhythm, you are revising for meaning at the same time.

We've taken this passage about as far as it will go, but one problem still remains. The rhythm seems okay (try it, as always, by reading it aloud with emphasis and coloration), but both sentences run to about the same length. For this reason, the one that follows this passage ought to be either much longer or very short.

When prose is read aloud, sentence shape presents fewer problems. The voice can shape and punctuate as it goes along. But when the voice atrophies, the eye does not make the same demands with equal insistence, and the larger shaping rhythms that build through a paragraph tend to blur—a problem hard to see and hard to remedy.

IT WOULD BE MUCH EASIER ON A VIDEO DISPLAY

We've been revising big chunks of prose. I know it seems dry and hard to follow. What we need is a big screen and a sound track to match, where we can *see* the patterns emerging. Since we don't have that here, I'm asking you, as Prologue does in *Henry V*, to "piece out our imperfections with your thoughts," to "Think, when we talk of horses, that you see them/Printing their proud hoofs i' th' receiving earth." You can reckon the cost of shapeless prose by the pain you feel in reading it, the choking sensation you feel as you try to digest these great lumps of peanut-butter prose. Let's go back to some smaller examples for relief and, as a treat, look at some good examples too. (Perhaps, recalling the example above, it will improve our theorizing!)

Here's easy pickings:

> However that may be, the importance of the term for my present purposes is that it does introduce at least some aspects of the concept of political equality into the arena of political discussion in the fifth century B.C.

The mixture as before:

> However that may be,
> the importance of the term for my present purposes **is that**
> it does introduce
> *at* least some aspects
> *of* the concept
> *of* political equality
> *into* the arena
> *of* political discussion
> *in* the fifth century B.C.

You see a mind here (as it happens, a brilliant one) simply gabbling along, writing as the words come, checked by no reflective self-consciousness about shape, qualifying and qualifying and qualifying the assertion into lumpishness. With peanut-butter prose, pure subtraction offers the best first revision. Here's how we might demonstrate it on a video display:

> However ~~that may be~~,
> ~~the importance of~~ the term ~~for my present purposes is that~~
> ~~it~~ does introduce
> *~~at least some aspects~~*
> *of* the concept
> *of* political equality
> *into* ~~the arena~~

of political discussion
in the fifth century B.C.

This is better:

> However, the term does introduce the concept of political equal-
> ity into political discussion in the fifth century B.C. (LF 53%)

Now move the "however," into the sentence to avoid beginning the sentence on an offbeat. Cutting out the guff shows
us the incipient tautology of those two "political"s; get rid of
one. Delete B.C., since from the context it is clear. Reposition
"fifth century." Voilà:

> The term, however, does introduce "equality" into fifth-century
> political discussion. (LF 72%)

Or, we might leave in "political" as modifying "equality" and
delete it before "discussion." Either way, when you finish revising this sentence for shape, the meaning seems a little thin,
doesn't it? The Official Style is great at concealing tautological
thinking with verbal lard.

Here's a shopping bag from the history of biology:

> It is not only the layperson whose horizon will be greatly ex-
> tended by the study of the history of ideas in biology. Advances
> in many areas of biology are so precipitous at the present time
> that specialists can no longer keep up with the developments in
> areas of biology outside their own.

Familiar symptoms:

> It is not only the layperson whose horizon **will be** greatly ex-
> tended
>   *by* the study
>   *of* the history

> *of* ideas
> *in* biology.
> Advances
>   *in* many areas
>   *of* biology
> *are* so precipitous
>   *at* the present time
> that specialists can no longer keep up
>   *with* the developments
>   *in* areas
>   *of* biology
>   *outside* their own.

Familiar treatment:

> Biology is developing so fast now that its history enlightens not only the layperson but the professional biologist working in a special field. (LF 56%)

We've not only realized our statutory LF percentage (50%, ±5%), but, by attending to *shape*, we have reorganized the *thinking* as well. The real axis of the original sentence—the relationship between the history of biology and its current rapid development—now revolves around a causal core.

THE HUMAN/AIRPLANE INTERFACE

Here now are two passages about the relation between airplanes and human beings. The first one tells us how hard it is to measure the pain airplane noise inflicts on people.

> A singular quantitative classification of the individual human response to any given noise level from a particular noise source is not available by virtue of the human quality of the response.

A perfect formulaic Official Style sentence:

A singular quantitative classification

of the individual human response
to any given noise level
from a particular noise source

is not available

by virtue
of the human quality
of the response.

The Official Style strives to abolish people as well as their actions. Here, we must resynthesize them. From "individual human response" and "human quality of the response" we get **People.** From "any given noise level" and "particular noise source" we get **sounds.** So we have

People hear sounds differently.

Passing by without comment the writer's embarrassing confusion of "singular" and "single," we can complete the utterance with "No single measurement works." And putting the two together in a causal relationship:

Because people hear differently, no single measurement of sound works. (LF 68%)

But "works" sounds too abrupt. Maybe we can't avoid "is possible."

Because people hear differently, no single measurement of sound is possible.

Put the actor and the action into natural alignment, and everything else falls into place. The Official Style abolishes people and their actions; revision must always try to resurrect them. Now, because "no profit is where is no pleasure taken," here is a description of the human/airplane interface (as an Official Stylist might put it) which has some shape, some life.

> No, when the stresses are too great for the tired metal, when the ground-mechanic who checks the de-icing equipment is crossed in love and skimps his job, way back in London, Idlewild, Gander, Montreal; when those or many things happen, then the little warm room with propellers in front falls straight down out of the sky into the sea or onto the land, heavier than air, fallible, vain.

> (Ian Fleming, *Live and Let Die* [New York: Charter Books, 1987], pp. 150–151.)

Let me try to diagram and highlight the shape, so that you can see it:

No,
when the stresses are too great for the tired metal,
when the ground-mechanic who checks the de-icing equipment
   is *crossed in love*
   and *skimps his job,*
      way back in London,
         Idlewild,
            Gander,
               Montreal;
when those or many things happen,

then the little warm room with propellers in front falls straight down
   out of the sky
     into the sea or
       onto the land,

     heavier than air,
      fallible,
       vain.

Try reading this sentence aloud, using the diagrammed version as a text. Don't be afraid to add rests between prose measures, to use the pitch of your voice to underline the natural shapes of the individual phrases. Try it. Notice how the string of prepositional phrases ("out of," "into," "onto") here works *for* us because it is part of a climactic triplet series, one echoed by the sequence of adjectives ("heavier than air, fallible, vain") which closes the sentence. And how resonant and romantic those place names become ("London, Idlewild, Gander, Montreal"), strung out in a row like that. This kind of prose pleasure need not be restricted to novels. Why not in environmental impact statements as well?

NEWS FROM SOCAL

Here is a final instance of how shape and voice interact. In the original version, the student has written a prose that considers neither the eye nor the ear. You can make sense of it, but it doesn't give you any help. Try reading it aloud.

> As the cults expose one imposing aspect of the Southern Californian culture, the eminence and glamour of Hollywood reveal an essential part of the city and reflect an important character flaw in the people. The escapist nature of the people manifests itself through an examination of the influence of Hollywood on the inhabitants. The myth and prestige of Hollywood has been a vital instrument in attracting outsiders into the Los Angeles scene. The people that migrate into this region as a result of their dreams regarding Hollywood demonstrate a disillusionment with society.

The style stands at ludicrous odds with the subject, an Official Style describing a very unofficial Southern California; the comedy factor looms larger even than the lard factor. We'll take the revision sentence by sentence.

As the cults expose one imposing aspect of the Southern Californian culture, the eminence and glamour of Hollywood reveal an essential part of the city and reflect an important character flaw in the people. (34 words)

Where is the *root action* here? And who, or what, is doing it? The Official Style has taught this student that such things don't really matter. The sentence "sounds okay" after all, doesn't it? Mature and scholarly? If "imposing" jars your ears so soon after "expose," makes you think the two words must be somehow connected in meaning, just shut your eyes and ears as The Official Style recommends. And follow its advice about the verbs, too, by splitting the action into two verbs that mean the same thing: "expose" and "reveal." We'll use just one in the revision, and position it to make the action stand out.

Revision

Religious cults reveal one part of Southern California culture, Hollywood glamour quite another. (13 words; LF 62%)

The next sentence shows perfectly how the shopping-bag formula blurs the action. Let me highlight with italics all the incipient actions:

The *escapist* nature of the people *manifests* itself through an *examination* of the *influence* of Hollywood on the inhabitants.

The formula provides an excuse to stop thinking in midproblem. Who is *examining? Influencing?* You cannot tell what this sentence means unless you read the rest of the passage. A quick revision will focus the problem:

Original

The myth and prestige of Hollywood has been a vital instrument in attracting outsiders into the Los Angeles scene. The people that migrate into this region as a result of their dreams regarding Hollywood demonstrate a disillusionment with society. (39 words)

Revision

Hollywood has attracted a lot of disillusioned people. (8 words; LF 79%)

Once we see this meaning, the hopelessly confused causality of the puzzling sentence ("The escapist nature . . .") stands out even more. You don't need that sentence at all, of course, but since it is there, let's look at it further. Notice the magnitude of the error it embodies.

The escapist nature of the people manifests itself through an examination of the influence of Hollywood on the inhabitants.

Cause and effect have been reversed, for a start. The "escapist nature manifests itself through an examination" really means that the "examination reveals the escapist nature." The action flows in the opposite direction. The writer goes on to say that Hollywood attracts a lot of disillusioned people from elsewhere. Again the direction of causality has been reversed: they are influencing Hollywood, not being influenced by it. I am beating this dead sentence to make a vital point: when you reverse cause and effect, *you are making a big mistake.* Imagine a military historian saying not "The tank revolutionized infantry warfare" but "Infantry warfare revolutionized the tank." Or an American historian who, instead of "Electricity liberated the farm housewife," wrote "The farm housewife liberated electricity." Yet our chronicler of Hollywood doesn't even know this mistake has been made. Prisoner of The Official Style, he or she just goes on because it fits the formula, "sounds right," and—Oh frabjous day!—generates a lot of words in a long line *of* strings *of* prepositional phrases *of* various types *in* The Official Style *of* writing used *in* academic departments *in* universities *of* higher learning *in* the United States *of* America.

PM ENLARGED

I've used reading aloud in this book as the simplest kind of self-diagnostic tool. It slows us down, makes us read with care instead of speed-reading the prose out of focus, as The Official Style encourages us to do. Reading aloud and with care, and several times, makes prose opaque rather than transparent, makes you look *at* the words rather than *through* them to a meaning glimpsed hastily in passing.

With this technique in mind, we can now add two more diagnostic procedures to our Paramedic Method:

1. Circle the prepositions.
2. Circle the "is" forms.
3. Ask, "Where's the action?" "Who's kicking who?"
4. Put this "kicking" action in a simple (not compound) active verb.
5. Start fast—no slow windups.
6. Write out the sentence on a blank sheet of paper and look at its shape.
7. Read the sentence aloud with emphasis and feeling.

With this expanded diagnostic repertoire, we go on to consider sentence sound and rhythm in more detail in the following chapter.

CHAPTER 3

SENTENCE LENGTH, RHYTHM, AND SOUND

The elements of prose style—grammar, syntax, shape, rhythm, emphasis, level, usage—all work as dependent variables. Change one and you change the rest. Rhythm and sound seem, for most prose writers, the most dependent of all. They affect nothing and everything affects them. They do affect something, though. They affect us. Rhythm constitutes the most vital of prose's vital life signs. Rhythmless, unemphatic prose always indicates that something has gone wrong.

TIN EARS

Tin Ears, insensitivity to the sound of words, indicate that the hearing that registers rhythm has been turned off. Tin Ears have become so common that often you can't tell mistakes from mindlessness. Was this sentence written tongue in cheek or just wax in ears?

> Conflict, chaos, competition, and combat combine to constitute both the labor and fertilizer of war and the fruit of this is honor.

Too resolute an alliteration, too many "c's":

> **C**onflict, **c**haos, **c**ompetition, and **c**ombat **c**ombine to **c**onstitute both the labor and fertilizer of war and the fruit of this is honor.

And "*f*ertilizer" and "*f*ruit" doesn't help, either. "Conflict" is a near synonym for "combat" and overlaps with "competition"; if you use "constitute" you don't need "combine." Nor does "this" refer to anything specific. Yet the sentence conceals a rhythm waiting for liberation. A little subtle subtraction leads to this:

> Combat, competition, and chaos constitute the fertilizer of war and the fruit of this fertilizer is honor.

One further change—"constitute the fertilizer of" = "fertilize"—yields a sentence with a sound and shape of its own:

> Combat, competition, and chaos fertilize war and produce its fruit—honor. (LF 50%)

We've kept the alliterative yoking of the opening triplet phrase and created a rhythmically emphatic place of honor for—*honor*.

The Official Style, deaf and blind, manages to create rhythm and shape only by accident. So, for example, a U.S. attorney refuses to talk about a controversial spy case with commendable, if desperate, pertinacity:

> I can't comment. We will not comment. We are not going to comment.

This three-segment climax has been used since classical times (when it was called *tricolon crescens*, each of the three elements being slightly longer than the previous one and thus building to a climax) as part of a sentence strategy for building long rhythmic periodic sentences. Winston Churchill was especially fond of it:

> Victory at all costs, victory in spite of all terror, victory however long and hard the road may be . . .

> This is not the end. It is not even the beginning of the end. But it is, perhaps, the end of the beginning.

The Official Style creates Tin Ears and when the ear atrophies, any hope of colloquial emphasis or climax goes down the drain. But when there is a voice to begin with, things are much easier to fix. Look at this flawed diamond:

> There is not a sign of life in the whole damned paper (with the possible exception of line 72).

A cinch to fix. Just reverse the order.

> With the possible exception of line 72, there is not a sign of life in the whole damn paper.

Terrific!

CHANGE-UPS

Sometimes you can see a colloquial voice change abruptly to an Official Style one: "This point just emphasizes the need of repeated experience for properly utilizing the various sense modalities." The sentence breaks in half after "experience." We expect a finish like, "to use all the senses," and get instead an Official Style translation. Here is a scholar doing the same thing, this time from sentence to sentence:

Official Style

The establishment of an error detection mechanism is necessary to establish a sense of independence in our own movement planning and correction.

Change-up

Plain English

Unless we know we are doing something wrong, we can't correct it.

Change-ups like this emphasize the voicelessness of The Official Style.

Voice seems to have been squeezed out of student prose by The Official Style. Here's an exception, a geography paper with real ears:

> Twice daily, at sunrise and sunset, a noisy, smoke-ridden train charges into the stillness of the Arabian desert. Winding about the everchanging windblown sand dunes, the "Denver Zephyr" not only defies the fatal forces of the notorious deserts, but for the non-native, offers an extraordinary encounter with the tightly closed Saudi society.

The "s" assonance—sunrise, sunset, noisy, smoke-ridden, stillness—seems to work, and so does "fatal forces," and "forces" echoes part of notorious which, with "deserts," defines those forces. The sentence allows the voice a full tonal range, a chance for pitch to rise and fall, and a chance to build a climax on "tightly closed Saudi society" as well. This expanded tonal range, alas, went unappreciated by the instructor: the paper was marked down for being too "journalistic." No good deed goes unpunished.

I'm suggesting that writers should become self-conscious about the sound of words. Once our ears have had their consciousness raised, they'll catch the easy problems as they flow from the pen—"however clever" will become "however shrewd" in the first draft—and the harder ones will seem easier to revise.

ARRHYTHMIA ATTACKS

Here are some arrhythmia attacks from a recent batch of papers. The first illustrates the power of a single verb—or lack of one.

> Reputation is also a serious consideration for native Trojans.

Why not:

> Trojans worship Reputation. (LF 66%)

The wordiness of the following sentence lends it an unintended faintly lubricious air:

> The first duty of female characters in the drama of this period is to illustrate the various dimensions of the male protagonist.

Why not:

> In the drama of this period female characters must above all illuminate the male protagonist. (LF 36%)

And how about

> Both film and song ask the eternal questions of young adulthood

as a revision of

> A good measure of this appeal can be traced to the fact that both the visual medium of the film and aural medium of the song confront the young person with eternal questions of young adulthood. (LF 69%)

The revision, by keeping the sentence short, preserves the natural ending emphasis for "young adulthood," and thus gives the voice someplace to go. Try reading both aloud several times. See what I mean?

Here's a businessman telling us about his firm's new health plan:

> When the sorting of the various problems was taking place, additional vitamins were introduced, cocktails reduced to a minimum, and a regular exercise program begun.

A natural *tricolon crescens* springs forth:

> While the plan was being started up, we took vitamins, cut down on the booze, and began a regular exercise program.

THE PARAMEDIC METHOD — FULL FORM

Often, when dealing with The Official Style, we must try revising a passage even if we are not sure what it means. In such cases, we may begin to understand the special terms just by trying to fathom their relationship. Practice such a "naive analysis," a "revise-to-understand exercise" on the following wonderfully arrhythmic sentence from a book about rhythm!

> Rhythm is that property of a sequence of events in time which produces in the mind of the observer the impression of proportion between the directions of the several events or groups of events of which the sequence is composed.

Look at what the prepositional-phrase strings do to the rhythm:

Rhythm **is** that property
   of a sequence
   of events

in time
which produces
 in the mind
 of the observer the impression
 of proportion
 between the directions
 of the several events or groups
 of events
 of which the sequence is composed.

Can you revise in a way to show that the writer has mastered her subject as well as written about it? Can you use the revision to clarify what the writer has obscured, drag her meaning from the depths of her prose? Try it. Here's the full form of the Paramedic Method to help:

1. Circle the prepositions.
2. Circle the "is" forms.
3. Ask, "Who's kicking who?" "Where's the action?"
4. Put this "kicking" action in a simple (not compound) active verb.
5. Start fast—no slow windups.
6. Write out each sentence on a blank sheet of paper and mark off its basic rhythmic units with a "/."
7. Read the passage aloud with emphasis and feeling.
8. Mark off sentence lengths in the passage with a "/."

Sentence length is one of the easiest PM tests to apply. Take a piece of your prose and a red pencil and draw a slash after every sentence. Two or three pages ought to make a large enough sample. If the red marks occur at regular intervals, you have, as they used to say in the Nixon White House, a problem. You can chart the problem another way, if you like. Choose a standard length for one sentence and then do a bar graph. If it looks like this,

---

47

———————————
————————————————
——————————————
————————————————
—————————————————————
——————————
——————————————————————————
————————

dandy. If like this,

——————————
———————————
—————————
———————————
—————————
———————————

not so dandy. Obviously, no absolute quantitative standards exist for how much variety is good, how little bad, but the principle couldn't be easier. Vary your sentence lengths. Naturally enough, complex patterns will fall into long sentences and emphatic conclusions work well when short. But no rules prevail except Avoid Monotony.

Here is a passage which certainly obeys this inviolable rule. It comes from a brilliantly written World War II memoir by Brendan Phibbs, *The Other Side of Time*. Dr. Phibbs has been talking about the self-dramatizing, self-serving American General George Patton, and moves from there to Patton's mirror opposite, General Lucien Truscott:

> And now, we said more happily, consider . . . Truscott. . . . Men like this are stamped, early in life, and the outlines of the mold spell honesty. They fill the mold without effort; it fits them and they have no question about who they are and what

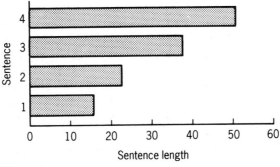

Figure 1

they can do. They're free of the need to grimace and prance; they're free to spend themselves on a cause, for an ideal, scorning advantage and chaining the ego in some remote corner to babble and shriek and rattle its shackles. Having won, they're satisfied with the achievement; they're not driven to seek their value in the gaze and the wonder of others, and they walk off into the quiet corners of history where the truth lives, grinning to watch imposters scribbling their worthless names across the walls of the public baths.

The quiet corners of history where the truth lives—what a wonderful phrase. Now, what creates the rhythm here? The sense of authentic voice? Of sentences with a shape which energizes meaning? Well, we might start with rule 8 of the PM, sentence length. Let's graph them. Such graphing is much easier when you write on an electronic screen; simple and cheap graphing programs lie ready to hand (see figure 1).

A varied, climactic sentence length—but that only begins to describe how it works. Let's apply rule 6, and mark off basic rhythmic units.

And now, we said more happily, consider . . . Truscott. . . . Men like this are stamped, / early in life, / and the outlines of the mold spell / honesty. / They fill the mold without effort; / it fits them / and they have no question about who they are / and what they can do. / They're free of the need to grimace and prance; / they're free to spend themselves on a cause, / for an ideal, / scorning advantage / and chaining the ego / in some remote corner / to babble and shriek and rattle its shackles. / Having won, / they're satisfied with the achievement; / they're not driven to seek their value in the gaze and the wonder of others, / and they walk off into the quiet corners of history where the truth lives, / grinning to watch imposters scribbling their worthless names / across the walls of the public baths.

What do the rhythmic units look like when diagrammed?

Men like this are stamped, /
early in life, /
and the outlines of the mold spell /
honesty. /
They fill the mold without effort; /
it fits them /
and they have no question about who they are /
and what they can do. /
They're free of the need to grimace and prance; /
they're free to spend themselves on a cause, /
for an ideal, /
scorning advantage /
and chaining the ego /
in some remote corner /
to babble and shriek and rattle its shackles. /
Having won, /
they're satisfied with the achievement; /
they're not driven to seek their value in the gaze and the wonder
    of others, /
and they walk off into the quiet corners of history where the
    truth lives, /
grinning to watch imposters scribbling their worthless names /
across the walls of the public baths.

I don't claim such a division is linguistically correct, whatever that might mean. Just the opposite. It is a quick and easy method any of us can use to chart our own reading of a passage, to see how our voice might embody the prose rhythm. Charting makes us specify, *become self-conscious about*, our own rhythmic interpretation. There's no better way to see how sentence rhythm and shape work than to use rules 6 through 8 of the PM. Here they are again:

6. Write out each sentence on a blank sheet of paper and mark off its basic rhythmic units with a "/."
7. Read the passage aloud with emphasis and feeling.
8. Mark off sentence lengths in the passage with a "/."

What have they told us here? Well, that the basic rhythmic units, at least as I see them, vary markedly in length. Second, that the passage invites stress on a series of crucial words. Again, let me show you what I mean:

Men like this are stamped, /
early in life, /
and the outlines of the mold spell /
honesty. /
They fill the mold without effort; /
it fits them /
and they have no question about who they are /
and what they can do. /
They're free of the need to grimace and prance; /
they're free to spend themselves on a cause, /
for an ideal, /
scorning advantage /
and chaining the ego /
in some remote corner /
to babble and shriek and rattle its shackles. /
Having won, /
they're satisfied with the achievement; /

they're not driven to seek their value in the gaze and the wonder
   of others, /
and they walk off into the quiet corners of history where
   the truth lives, /
grinning to watch imposters scribbling their worthless names /
across the walls of the public baths.

The PM lends itself naturally to the typographic expressivity of an electronic screen. The two work together to give anyone who cares about prose the power to analyze how a passage really works. The simple typographical diagram I've just invented here immediately tells us more about the passage. It builds toward a definite climax in a memorable phrase, sets up a strong emphasis on honesty, and develops from that a meditation that ends up being about the quiet corners of history where the truth lives. And notice how many strong verb forms, how many actions, the passage contains?

Stamped
Spell honesty
Fill the mold
What they can *do*
grimace and *prance*
spend themselves on a cause
chaining the ego
babble and *shriek* and *rattle* its shackles
Having *won*
driven to *seek*
walk off into the quiet corners
grinning to *watch* imposters
scribbling their worthless names

The passage recreates for us how history is both acted and reenacted, how it happens and how we seek its truth, waiting there for us in quiet corners. Phibbs wants to describe how we respond to social situations, how we elicit *from* them what we bring *to* them.

Here, by way of contrast, is a passage of genuinely awesome arrhythmic unintelligibility from an American sociologist. It talks about, as the editor explains—inasmuch as it has been given me to understand him, much less the sociologist—the background expectancies of situations which make social interaction possible. That is to say, it covers—I think—much the same ground as the Phibbs passage.

> The properties of indexical expressions and indexical actions are ordered properties. These consist of organizationally demonstrable sense, or facticity, or methodic use, or agreement among "cultural colleagues." Their ordered properties consist of organizationally demonstrable rational properties of indexical expressions and indexical actions. Those ordered properties are ongoing achievements of the concerted commonplace activities of the investigators. The demonstrable rationality of indexical expressions and indexical actions retains over the course of its managed production by members the character of ordinary, familiar, routinized, practical circumstances.

Does it *have* to be this way? Or is such Official Style prose itself a kind of professional grimacing and prancing? Using the PM as your guide, contrast the two passages. They make a revealing pair.

I've not found a really satisfactory way to indicate prose rhythm in a printed book. But try reading aloud these two passages we've just examined, one after the other. Don't hurry. And don't read them in a monotone. Let the pitch and timbre of your voice vary. Try out various combinations of pitch, stress, and timing. (There are several ways to read the Phibbs passage, for example.) You can mark pitch variation with a wavy up-and-down line above the text, for a start. And mark musical rests (#, ##, ###) after each phrase and sentence. Try reading each passage aloud and having someone else time you, observe where you pause and for how long. The first passage projects a recognizable voice; it is literally "readable."

The second passage, academic prose at its most voiceless, is obviously meant to be read—skimmed—silently.

A VOICE FROM THE 60S

Prose varies widely in the kind of performance instructions that it gives. Official Style academic prose gives very few such instructions. The voice has nowhere to go, no natural place to rise and fall, hurry and pause. Metronome prose: tick-tock, tick-tock, tick-tock. Here, for extreme contrast, is a trip down prose nostalgia lane that offers lots of performance instructions. A sociology professor has taped a hippie guru telling us what it was like up at Big Sur in the 60s. Try marking the performance instructions; underline, double underline, use quotation marks, whatever.

When I first got up there, it was a real romantic kind of picture. Man, it was kind of foggy. There were those really beautiful people—men, women, kids, dogs and cats, and campfires. It seemed quiet and stable. And I really felt like love was about me. I thought, "This is the place, man. It was happening. I don't have to do it. I would just kind of fit in and do my thing and that would be like a groove."

After we were there about fifteen or twenty minutes, I heard the people bitching and moaning. I listened to it for a while and circulated around to hear more about it, and, man, I couldn't believe it. Here they were secure in their land—beautiful land, where they could be free—and all these people were doing was bitching and moaning. I thought, "Oh, shit, man! Do I have to go into this kind of shit again where I gotta step in and get heavy and get ratty and get people to start talking? Do I have to get them to be open and get in some dialogue and get some communication going and organization? What the——is wrong with the leadership here, that this kind of state of affairs is happening? And why do I have to do it again? Man, I'm through with it. I just got through with hepatitis and double pneumonia and . . .——it!" Then I really felt bad.

(Lewis Yablonsky, *The Hippie Trip* [New York: Pegasus, 1968], p. 91.)

This is speech, for a start. Hippie speech, heavily syncopated speech, sliding quickly over interim syllables from heavy stress to heavy stress: "first," "romantic," "foggy," "really," "love." Once you know the syncopated pattern, it is easy to mark up a passage like this. But if you don't know the pattern? Imagine yourself a foreigner trying to read this passage with a natural emphasis. It does sometimes give natural rhythmic clues. "This is the *place*, man. It was *happening*. I don't *have* to do it." The arrangement of the words underscores the sense—the scene has become the actor and the actor the scene. So, too, the alliterative repetition of "go into," "gotta step in," "get heavy," "get ratty," "get people" gives us a clear performance clue. But the passage by itself does not include a full guide to its performance. (You needed to be part of the scene to talk this talk like a native. Hippie speech was an *argot*, a special way of speaking used to dramatize a special way of living. The guru just quoted hadn't always talked this way. I know—he was in my class at Yale before the 60s "came down.")

A PERIODIC GUIDE TO PROSE PERFORMANCE

How can prose include a performance guide, anyway? In the past, it has done so most often by a very different route, by building up patterns of repetition, balance, antithesis, and parallelism. This package of systemic controls, usually called a "periodic sentence," has been the traditional way to control a long, complex sentence since classical Greek. The periodic style has been what we might call the "good" Official Style in Western stylistic history. It has striven for the official attributes of public formality, authoritative impressiveness, solemnity even, but in a way that *emphasizes* voice rather than etiolating it. It thus represents true solemnity, a counterstatement to the kind of prose we have been revising. It *designs* a long sentence under strict control, not one stuffed with words. Any discussion of The Official Style should consider at least one instance of its legitimate ancestor. The following example comes from Lord Brougham (1778–1868), the most famous parliamentary orator of his day, in his speech defending Queen Caroline in the divorce proceedings George IV had brought against her. This kind of prose seems fulsome to us, but notice how many performance clues it contains.

> But, my lords, I am not reduced to this painful necessity. I feel that if I were to touch this branch of the case now, until any event shall afterwards show that unhappily I am deceiving myself—I feel that if I were now to approach the great subject of recrimination, I should seem to give up the higher ground of innocence on which I rest my cause; I should seem to be justifying when I plead Not Guilty; I should seem to argue in extenuation and in palliation of offences, or levities, or improprieties, the least and the lightest of which I stand here utterly to deny. For it is false, as has been said—it is foul and false as those have dared to say, who, pretending to discharge the higher duties to God, have shown that they know not the first of those duties to their fellow-creatures—it is foul, and false, and scandalous in those who have said (and they know that it is so who have dared to say) that there are improprieties admitted in the conduct of the Queen. I deny that the admission has been made. I contend that the evidence does not prove them. I will show you that the evidence disproves them. One admission, doubtless, I do make; and let my learned friends who are of counsel for the Bill take all the benefit of it, for it is all that they have proved by their evidence.

Several powerful variables contend in a prose like this. The patterning aims above all to establish a tone of high seriousness. But look at it simply for performance clues. It tells us exactly how it ought to be performed. Shape and sound coincide. It builds to a climactic central assertion and then tapers off. Perhaps a diagram will help:

But, my lords,
I am not reduced to this painful necessity.
I feel that if
I were to touch this branch of the case now, until
any event shall afterwards show that unhappily
I am deceiving myself—
I feel that if
I were now to approach the great subject of
recrimination,
I should seem to give up the higher ground of
innocence on which
I rest my cause;
I should seem to be justifying when
I plead Not Guilty;
I should seem to argue in extenuation
and in palliation of
offences, or improprieties, the least and
the lightest of which
I stand here utterly to deny.
For it is false, as has been said—
it is foul and false as those have dared to say
who, pretending to discharge
the higher duties to God,
have shown that they know not
the first of those duties to their fellow creatures—
it is foul, and false, and scandalous
in those who have said
(and they know that it is so
who have dared to say)
THAT THERE ARE IMPROPRIETIES ADMITTED IN
    THE CONDUCT OF THE QUEEN.
I deny that the admission has been made.
I contend that the evidence does not prove them.

> I will show you that the evidence disproves them.
> One admission, doubtless, I do make;
> and let my learned friends who are
> of counsel for the Bill
> Take *all* the benefit of *it*, for *it* is *all* that they have
> proved by their evidence.

Notice how the conclusion is handled? He uses a chiasmus (an *ab : ba* pattern) to fold the last clause back up upon itself and then uses the last prepositional phrase to end the whole rhythmic unit. And the main pattern stands clear. First a series of repetitive hammer-blow assertions; next a set of balanced assertions and rebuttals; then the central point; then a short return to the first pattern and a short return to the second; then the final chiasmus.

We don't write prose like this anymore (although advertising copywriters certainly love chiasmus!). But whether you relish it as I do or not, you ought to try in your own writing to give equally good performance instructions, and, in your long sentences, to maintain equally good syntactic and stylistic control. For, again, that is what sentence length, rhythm, and sound are—a series of instructions, of controls, for how your sentence should be performed. And if your reader takes pleasure in performing your prose, you have her on your side. She is acting in your play.

We've seen how sentences become shapeless when the voice goes out of them. Prose that is not voiced becomes shapeless and unemphatic in the same way that an unexercised muscle loses its tone. And it works the other way, too. If we do not look at a piece of prose, try to perform it, we'll cease to hear real voices, our own and others', when we speak. Writing and speaking form a spiral. If they intensify each other, the spiral goes up. If they don't, each drives the other down.

CHAPTER 4

THE OFFICIAL STYLE

Up to now we've concentrated on translating The Official Style into plain English. Now, we focus on the style itself. And, instead of simply condemning it, we'll ask how and why it has come about, how it works in the world.

Students of style have traditionally distinguished three basic levels—high, middle, low. The content of these categories varied somewhat, but usually the high style was a formal and ornamental style for a solemn and ritualized occasion, a style like Lord Brougham's. The low style enshrined the loose and sloppy intercourse of daily life, a style like the hippie guru's. And the middle style stood somewhere in between, Brendan Phibbs's carefully crafted sentences being an excellent example. Since World War II, American prose has worked a pronounced variation on this enduring pattern. The low style, an affair now largely of *viva-voce* communication, has pretty much disintegrated into a series of "I-mean-like-you-know" shrugs and spastic tics, where I go, "like," and you go, "you know?" And since we have come to suspect fancy clothes and formal ceremony as undemocratic, we have come to suspect a high style like Brougham's, too. We think of it as "only rhetoric."

As a substitute for both, we've clasped to our bosoms The Official Style—a style that is formal without ever pretending to be grand. The Official Style is often stigmatized as bureaucratese or jargon, and it often is both. But it is a genuine style, and one that reflects the genuine bureaucratization of American life. It has its own rules and its own ambitions, and everyone today must grapple with them. The Official Style comes to us in many guises but two main ones: as the language of the learned professions and as the language of bureaucracy, whether in government, business, or the military. The learned professions want above all to sound learned and scientific—disinterested, impersonal, factual. Bureaucracy wants above all to sound official—neutral, formal, authoritative, inevitable. Both ambitions converge on a common set of verbal habits, The Official Style.

The Official Style runs from school days to retirement. As soon as you realize that you live "in a system," whether P.S. 41, the University of California, the Department of Agriculture, General Motors, or the Army Signal Corps, you start developing The Official Style. Used unthinkingly, it provides the quickest tip-off that you have become system-sick and look at life only through the system's eyes. It is a scribal style, ritualized, formulaic, using a special vocabulary to describe a special kind of world, the world of bureaucratic officialdom. And it is, increasingly, the only kind of prose style many Americans ever encounter. It is also, along with the social changes that sponsor it, one of the main reasons for our prose problem. The low style has dissolved, the high style has hardened and dehydrated, and the middle style has simply evaporated. The Official Style threatens to replace all three.

If you can analyze, write, and translate it, maybe you can find your niche in the system—public sector or private—without losing your soul to it. For you may have to write in The

Official Style, but you don't have to think in it. If you are the first on the scene after the sports car has missed the curve, climbed the hedge, and ended up on the lawn, you won't ask the driver, as did one policeman, "How, uh, sir, did you achieve this configuration?"

THE OFFICIAL BOA

Sometimes you can see The Official Style seizing its prey like a boa constrictor and gradually squeezing the life out of it. Here's a college student first feeling its grip.

> Twelve-year-old boys like to fight. Consequently, on several occasions I explained to them the negative aspects of fighting. Other responsibilities included keeping them dry (when near the creek or at times of rain), seeing that they bathed, attending to any minor wounds they acquired, and controlling their mischievous behavior. Another responsibility was remaining patient with the children.

The first sentence says simply what it has to say. The second sentence starts to sound like a report. It strives for a needless explicitness ("on several occasions") and it aims for a pseudoscientific neutrality of description ("the negative aspects of fighting"). To remain on the same stylistic level as the first sentence, it ought to read, "So, I often told them to stop." "Other responsibilities included" is the language of a job description. The frantic scramble of summer camp life is being viewed through a personnel form. The prose is scary as well as stilted because life has been reduced to something that will fit in a file cabinet. Only on official forms do small boys "acquire minor wounds" or counselors "attend" them. In life, they cut themselves and you give them a Band-Aid. In life, you keep them out of the creek and out of the rain, instead of "keeping them dry (when near the creek or at times of rain)." And, instead of "controlling their mischievous behavior," you make them behave or even give them a kick in the pants. As for "Another responsibility was remaining patient with the children," that translates into, "I had to keep my temper." If the writer had stayed on the stylistic level he began with, he would have written:

> Twelve-year-old boys like to fight. Often, I had to stop them. And I had to keep them out of the rain, and the creek, and mischief generally. I had to give out Band-Aids and keep my temper. (LF 35%)

Why didn't he? You don't write The Official Style by nature. It has to be learned. Why did he fall into it here? He was *applying for* something. And you apply for something—in this case, admission to medical school—on a form. And a form requires an official style. The Official Style. It makes what you've done sound important and, still more important than important, Official.

Ever since George Orwell's famous essay "Politics and the English Language" (1946), The Official Style has been interpreted as a vast conspiracy to soften our minds and corrupt our political judgment. Social science jargon has been seen as pure hokum, an attempt to seem more scientific than you are. And the language of Pentagon bureaucrats usually combines the worst of the civil bureaucracy and the military high command. The Orwell conspiracy theory is sometimes true, but not the whole truth. We all want to fit in, to talk the language of the country. This desire is what keeps society glued together. So the impulses that attract us to The Official Style are not always perverse or depraved. Just the opposite. They are the primary social impulses. And so when we analyze The Official Style, we're really talking about how we live now, about our society as well as our prose, about how to survive in the system. What does the prose tell us about the society?

Euphemism and Evasion

Well, it is a euphemistic society, for a start. It thinks of every town dump as a "sanitary landfill site," every mentally retarded child as "exceptional," every dog catcher as an "animal welfare officer," every pigpen as a "unitary hog-raising facility." Society may have its pains and problems, but language can sugarcoat them. An Official Stylist would never say an area was so polluted that plants obviously couldn't grow there. Instead: "Natural biotic habitats are conspicuously absent from the region."

And it is a society with a voracious press, so that officials often have to say something when they have nothing to say, or nothing they *can* say. So when a State Department spokesman was asked how the conference is going, he did not say "God knows!" but instead:

> I think it is already possible that this particular summit is one that is on the way to a substantial result. There has been evidence of an encouragingly large area of agreement toward a concrete and concerted action program by the various countries represented here—a program that will be concise and meaningful in its nature.

The Official Style society is also a society afraid of taking responsibility. The system acts, not the people within it. If its first rule is "Never call anything by its right name," its second is "Keep your head down. Don't assert anything you'll have to take the blame for. Don't, if you can help it, assert anything at all." Anthony Sampson, in his *Anatomy of Britain*, has culled a few examples of this supercaution from the more courtly British Civil Service version of The Official Style and supplied plain-language translations.

> We hope that it is fully appreciated that . . .
> You completely fail to realize that . . .

63

Greater emphasis should be laid on . . .
   You haven't bothered to notice . . .

We have the impression that insufficient study has been given
to . . .
   No one has considered . . .

Our enquiry seemed to provide a welcome opportunity for dis-
cussions of problems of this kind . . .
   No one had thought of that before . . .

We do not think that there is sufficient awareness . . .
   There is ignorance . . .

There has been a tendency in the past to overestimate the possibilities of useful short-term action in public investment . . .
   You should look ahead . . .

There should be an improvement in the arrangements to enable
ministers to discharge their collective responsibility.
   The cabinet should work together.

The rule is clear. Don't assert anything you can get tagged
with later. It may come back to haunt you. So never write "I
think" or "I did." Keep the verbs passive and impersonal: "It
was concluded that" or "Appropriate action was initiated on
the basis of systematic discussion indicating that." Often, as
with politicians being interviewed on TV, The Official Style
aims deliberately at saying nothing at all, but saying it in the
required way. Or at saying the obvious impressively. The Official Stylist must seem in control of everything but responsible
for nothing. Thus a member of Congress, instead of saying
that the government will listen to consumer complaints, says
that it will "review existing mechanisms of consumer input,
thruput, and output and seek ways of improving these linkages
via consumer consumption channels." The Official Style has
seized upon the computer language of *input, output,* and *interface* as a magical poetic diction, a body of sacred and intrinsi-
cally beautiful metaphors. Thus a U.S. senator indicted on

bribery charges does not ask the advice of his friends. Instead, bathing in computer charisma, he is "currently receiving personal and political input from my supporters and friends throughout the state."

It is often hard to tell with The Official Style how much is self-conscious put-on and how much is real ineptitude, genuine system-sickness. Students often suspect that the length and physical weight of their papers are more important than what they say, yet it is not only in school that papers are graded thus. Here is a famous Washington lawyer, talking about legal language:

> In these days when every other type of professional report, good or poor, is dressed up in a lovely ringed and colored plastic binder, some people still are prone to judge legal performance quantitatively by verbal volume. Thirty years ago two of us answered a difficult and intricate legal problem by concisely writing: "Gentlemen, after examining the statute in your state, all analogous statutes, and all of the cases, we have concluded that what you want to do is lawful." That client was not happy; he went down to Wall Street, got the same opinion backed by thirty turgid typewritten pages, and felt much more comfortable.

> (Quoted in Joseph C. Guelden's *The Superlawyers* [New York: Weybright and Talley, 1972], p. 306.)

HAMLET AND HOG PRICES

It is not only bureaucrats who find length and obscurity impressive. Here is another example of The Official Style inflating something short and sweet:

> A policy decision inexorably enforced upon a depression-prone individual whose posture in respect to his total psychophysical environment is rendered antagonistic by apprehension or by inner-motivated disinclination for ongoing participation in human exis-

tence is the necessity for effectuating a positive selection between two alternative programs of action, namely, (a) the continuance of the above-mentioned existence irrespective of the dislocations, dissatisfactions, and disabilities incurred in such a mode, or (b) the voluntary termination of such existence by self-initiated instrumentality, irrespective in this instance of the undetermined character of the subsequent environment, if any, in which the subject may be positioned as an end result of this irrevocable determination.

This must be a joke. In fact it is, one of the clever variations on common clichés by Richard D. Altick, a literary critic. He uses it in a marvellous book called *A Preface to Critical Reading*, the literary text varied is, of course, Hamlet's "To be or not to be, that is the question." It's fun and instructive to take a short familiar quotation and translate it into The Official Style. Pick something at random from a dictionary of quotations and try it. How about this, from *The Book of Common Prayer*? "Wine that maketh glad the heart of man; and oil to make him a cheerful countenance, and bread to strengthen man's heart." Or Miranda's famous declaration from Shakespeare's *Tempest*, "O brave new world, that hath such people in it." Or Tom Paine's "These are the times that try men's souls."

Now, for contrast, The Official Style from a real social scientist, an economist this time.

The evidence for the cobweb model lies in the quasi-periodic fluctuations in prices of a number of commodities. The hog cycle is perhaps the best known, but cattle and potatoes have sometimes been cited as others which obey the "theorem." . . . That the observed hog cycles were too long for the cobweb theorem was first observed in 1935 by Coase and Fowler (1935, 1937). The graph of cattle prices given by Ezekiel (1938) as evidence for the cobweb theorem implies an extraordinarily long period of production (5–7 years). The interval between successive peaks for other commodities tends to be longer than three production periods.

In the world of the triumphant MBA, businesspeople, especially, have to process reams of such prose. Fortunately for us, we have a translation of this particular passage by someone who understands it—a distinguished economist (and a wonderful prose stylist) named Donald McCloskey:

> The whole notion of the cobweb is based on the ups and downs of, say, hog prices. But hog prices take much longer to go up and down than it takes to raise hogs. Something is wrong. What is wrong, I'll venture, is that the irrational theory of how farmers make guesses about the future is mistaken. (LF 34%)
>
> (*The Rhetoric of Economics* [Madison: U. of Wisconsin P., 1985], p. 95.)

McCloskey has cut the passage down by a third, but he has done much more than that. He has changed its voice, or rather given it one. He has moved it from one rhetorical domain, The Official Style of economics and business, to another, less restrictive one, the middle style of ordinary written conversation, one which we can all share, which is to say, all understand. It may well be that writing like the revision would hurt your career chances as an economist, but isn't economics, as well as the rest of us, the poorer therefore?

You must, if you are to write prose in an America and a world fated to become ever more bureaucratic, learn how to use The Official Style, even perhaps how to enjoy it, without becoming imprisoned by it. You must manage to remember who is on first base, even if often you will not want to let on that you know. Long ago, La Rochefoucauld in his book of *Maxims* defined "a grave manner" as "a mysterious carriage of the body to cover defects of the mind." The Official Style has elevated this into an article of faith. Here is a sociological sample collected by Malcolm Cowley, with his translation:

> In effect, it was hypothesized that certain physical data categories including housing types and densities, land use characteristics, and ecological location constitute a scalable content area. This

could be called a continuum of residential desirability. Likewise, it was hypothesized that several social data categories, describing the same census tracts, and referring generally to the social stratification system of the city, would also be scalable. This scale would be called a continuum of socio-economic status. Thirdly, it was hypothesized that there would be a high positive correlation between the scale types on each continuum.

Here's the translation:

> Rich people live in big houses set further apart than those of poor people. By looking at an aerial photograph of any American city, we can distinguish the richer from the poorer neighborhoods. (LF 65%)

> ("Sociological Habit Patterns in Linguistic Transmogrification," *The Reporter*, September 20, 1956.)

Such prose seems to aim at being scientific but actually wants to be priestly, to cast a witch doctor's spell. To translate the prose into a plain style—that is, to revise it into ordinary English—breaks the spell and defeats the purpose. Revision here becomes an act of satire.

THE RETURN OF POETIC DICTION

We face the euphemistic habit again here, but on a larger scale this time. The Official Style always wants to make things seem better than they are, more mysterious and yet somehow more controlled, more inevitable. It strives, at all times, both to disarm and to impress us. It suggests that it sees the world differently—sees, even, a different world. It suggests that those who see in this way form a charmed circle. Now such a use of language does not, to students of literature, sound unfamiliar. It is called *poetic diction*. And this is what The Official Style amounts to—a kind of poetic diction. *Here we come to the main problem with The Official Style. There is no point in reproaching it for not being clear.* It does not really want to be clear. It wants to be *poetic*. At its best, it wants to tell you *how it feels to be an official*, to project the sense of numinous self-importance officialdom confers. It wants to make a prosaic world mysterious.

I know, I know. It doesn't do it very well. But that's not the point. Until we see what it is trying to do, we can neither understand it nor translate it with any pleasure. Maybe a comparison from another time and context will make the point clearer. Here is a series of plain-language translations of Official Style poetic diction that the English poet Alexander Pope compiled for a satire on false poetic sublimity called *Peri Bathous* (1728). He gives first the poetic diction and then the ordinary-language equivalent.

Poetic Diction	*Plain English*
For whom thus rudely pleads my loud-tongued gate, That he may enter . . .	Who knocks at the Door?
Advance the fringed curtains of thy eyes, And tell me who comes yonder . . .	See who is there.
The wooden guardian of our privacy Quick on its axle turn . . .	Shut the Door.

Bring me what Nature, tailor to the
     Bear,
 To Man himself denied: She gave me
     Cold
 But would not give me Clothes . . .
	Bring my Clothes.

Bring forth some remnant of the *Promethean* theft, Quick to expand th'inclement air congealed By *Boreas'* rude breath . . .	Light the Fire.

Yon Luminary amputation needs,   Snuff the Candle.
Thus shall you save its half-
    extinguished life.

Apply thine engine to the spongy door,   Uncork the Bottle and
Set *Bacchus* from his glassy prison free,   chip the Bread.
And strip white *Ceres* of her nut-
    brown coat.

And here is a modern version of such a list, culled from
an environmental impact statement filed by the FAA. I have
added the headings and the Plain English translation.

Poetic Diction	*Plain English*
limited in length	short
small faunal species	rats
experience growth	grow
annoyance factors	annoyances
police protection services	police
aircraft with lower noise emission characteristics	quieter planes
overlain by impervious surfaces	paved
exotic effluents	chemicals
weedy species	weeds
stepwise methodology	method
pollutant emissions control strategies	smog filters
olfactory impact	smell

Here is yet another glossary, an unintentional self-satire
this time, issued by the U.S. Office of Education (1971).
(Again, the headings are mine, but this time the Plain English
equivalents have been supplied by the Office of Education
itself, to prevent self-bewilderment.)

Poetic Diction	*Plain English*
Allocation of personnel and logistic resources to accomplish an identifiable objective. Activities constitute the basis for defining personnel assignments and for scheduling system operations.	Activity
The splitting of an entity into its constituent parts and the determination of relations among the parts and groups of the components.	Analysis
Production and refinement of a system or a product through trial-revision until it accomplishes its specified objectives.	Development
Those things (actions) that must be done to accomplish the overall job are referred to as functions.	Functions
To carry out. To fulfill. To give practical effect to and ensure actual fulfillment by concrete measures.	Implement
Enhanced performance on any important dimension without detriment to the other essential dimensions.	Improvement
The job to be done, be it a product, a completed service, or a change in the condition of something or somebody.	Mission
A discrepancy or differential between "what is" and "what should be" (i.e., "what is required" or "what is desired"). In educational planning, "need" refers to problems rather than solutions, to the student "product" rather than to the resources for achieving that product, to	Need

the ends of education rather than to the means for attaining those ends.

That toward which effort is directed. An intent statement and production for which a procedure is developed and resources allocated with a specific time frame and a measurable product signaling attainment.

Objectives

The organizational, procedural, technological, and support arrangements by which an agency has the capacity to apply problem-solving processes to any problem that it may face.

Planning Capability or Planning Competence

Elements of a function that, when performed by people and things in proper sequential order, will or should resolve the parent function. Tasks may be performed by people, equipment, or people/equipment combination.

Tasks

(Robert A. Watson, "Making Things Perfectly Clear," *Saturday Review*, July 24, 1971.)

Imagine trying to *think* in a world speaking this language—a world where the simplest human activity is translated immediately into its most abstract equivalent and then immediately tossed into this gooey marmalade of pretentious tautology? This particular bureaucratic glossary was issued in the name of clarity, but doesn't it aim obviously at something else entirely? Doesn't it yearn for a playful, poetic, *ornamental* use of language? Those who use The Official Style seldom acknowledge the paradox, but you must feel its truth if you are not to make grotesque mistakes. Clarity is often the last thing The Official Style really wants to create and, if you find yourself in a bureaucratic context, often the last thing you want to create. A sociology paper or a corporate memo in plain English could spell disaster. You may well want, in marshaling your thoughts, to write out an ordinary language version. But you must then translate it into The Official Style. You must, that is, learn to read, write, and translate The Official Style as if it were a foreign language. Play games with it by all means, but don't get fooled by it.

Bureaucrats have, in the past few years, begun to do just this—play games with it. One government official, Philip Broughton, created something called the "Systematic Buzz Phrase Projector." It consists of three columns of words:

Column 1	*Column 2*	*Column 3*
0. integrated	0. management	0. options
1. total	1. organizational	1. flexibility
2. systematized	2. monitored	2. capability
3. parallel	3. reciprocal	3. mobility
4. functional	4. digital	4. programming
5. responsive	5. logistical	5. concept
6. optional	6. transitional	6. time-phase
7. synchronized	7. incremental	7. projection
8. compatible	8. third generation	8. hardware
9. balanced	9. policy	9. contingency

(*Newsweek*, May 6, 1968.)

You think of any three numbers, 747 say, and then read off the corresponding words, "synchronized digital projection." It is a device to generate verbal ornament, a machine for poetic diction. In fact, computer programs for making poetry in just this random way now exist. Try making up a version for whatever special dialect of The Official Style you need to write. You can pick numbers the way you do for a lottery. Not only will it lend new resonance and authority to your prose, but it will act as a multiplier, increasing length and weight. It also acts as a mechanical muse, generates inspiration, or at least serviceable instant flapdoodle. Produce a phrase by the three-number procedure, invent a sentence for it, and then spend a paragraph or two reflecting on what it might mean. Invent a reality to which the phrase can refer.

A SOCIETY AFRAID OF BEING SUED

The deepest origins of The Official Style—and it flourished as far back as the Roman empire—lie in the language of the law. And, more especially, in the style of *statutes*, in legal language at its most Official, when it wants to be most numinous, most impressive, most priestly. This historical dimension of The Official Style has come to haunt American society as it becomes more and more litigious. We are all afraid of being sued. We think that if we write *statutorially*, we'll somehow not get sued, or at least not convicted. Yet this attempt at boilerplate almost always backfires. As with The Official Style, when you attempt to outlaw the playfulness of language, to *be clear and nothing else*, the poetic diction sneaks back in through the back door. We'll confront this contemporary problem, *the statutory temptation* we might call it, by looking at a section from the California Penal Code (Section 384a) which warns us not to pick the flowers along the freeway.

The general strategy of statutory argument is *iterative*; it wants to include, iterate, every possible case. Everything is to be spelled out, made perfectly clear, pushed beyond the need for interpretation. How does it work out in practice? Prose like this, though of immeasurable antiquity and precedent, often creates unintended effects.

> Every person who within the State of California willfully or negligently cuts, destroys, mutilates, or removes any tree or shrub, or fern or herb or bulb or cactus or flower, or huckleberry or redwood greens, or portion of any tree or shrub, or fern or herb or bulb or cactus or flower, or huckleberry or redwood greens, growing upon state or county highway rights-of-way, or

who removes leaf mold thereon; provided, however, that the provisions of this section shall not be construed to apply to any employee of the state or of any political subdivision thereof engaged in work upon any state, county or public road or highway while performing such work under the supervision of the state or of any political subdivision thereof, and every person who willfully or negligently cuts, destroys, mutilates or removes any tree or shrub, or fern or herb or bulb or cactus or flower, or huckleberry or redwood greens, growing upon public land or upon land not his own, or leaf mold on the surface of public land, or upon land not his own, without a written permit from the owner of the land signed by such owner or his authorized agent, and every person who knowingly sells, offers, or exposes for sale, or transports for sale, any tree or shrub, or fern or herb or bulb or cactus or flower, or huckleberry or redwood greens, or portion of any tree or shrub, or fern or herb or bulb or cactus or flower, or huckleberry or redwood greens, or leaf mold, so cut or removed from state or county highway rights-of-way, or removed from public land or from land not owned by the person who cut or removed the same without the written permit from the owner of the land, signed by such owner or his authorized agent, shall be guilty of a misdemeanor and upon conviction thereof shall be punished by a fine of not more than five hundred dollars ($500) or by imprisonment in a county jail for not more than six months or by both such fine and imprisonment.

See what happens? The repetitions begin to sound like the formulas of epic poetry, pushing the whole passage toward the high style. And these repetitions make the passage sound like an Eastern religious chant, with its endless repetition of identical phrases. And at the same time, the mechanical appearance of the repetition makes the nonlawyer laugh, pushes the whole passage toward the low style. This passage represents The Official Style at its most formulaic. You can see how near it comes to turning into poetry. Let's reformat it as such, to dramatize its formulary mystery:

Every person who
within the State of California

willfully or negligently
  cuts,
    destroys,
      mutilates, or
        removes

[chorus]

    any tree or shrub, or fern or herb or bulb or cactus or
    flower, or huckleberry or redwood greens,
        or portion of
    any tree or shrub, or fern or herb or bulb or cactus or
    flower, or huckleberry or redwood greens,

growing upon state or county highway rights-of-way, or
  who removes leaf mold thereon;

(provided, however, that

the provisions of this section shall not be construed to apply to
      any employee **of the state**
  or of any political subdivision thereof
engaged in work **upon any state,**
county or public road or highway while performing such work
  under the supervision **of the state**
  or of any political subdivision thereof),

and every person who
willfully or negligently
  cuts,
    destroys,
      mutilates, or
        removes

[chorus]

> any tree or shrub, or fern or herb or bulb or cactus or
> flower, or huckleberry or redwood greens,
> > or portion of
> any tree or shrub, or fern or herb or bulb or cactus or
> flower, or huckleberry or redwood greens,

growing upon public **land** or
> upon **land** not his **own**,
> or leaf mold on the surface
> of public **land**, or
> > upon **land** not his own,
without a written permit from the **owner**
> of the **land**
> > signed by such **owner**
> or his authorized agent,

and **every person who**
knowingly
> sells,
> > offers, or
> > > exposes for sale, or
> > > > transports for sale,

[chorus]

> any tree or shrub, or fern or herb or bulb or cactus or
> flower, or huckleberry or redwood greens,
> > or portion of
> any tree or shrub, or fern or herb or bulb or cactus or
> flower, or huckleberry or redwood greens, or leaf mold,

so cut or **removed** from state or county highway rights-of-way,
> or **removed** from public **land**
> > or from **land** not owned by the person
who cut or **removed** the same without the written permit from
> the **owner** of the **land**,
> signed by such **owner** or his authorized agent,

---

shall be guilty of a misdemeanor
and upon conviction thereof
shall be punished
> **by** a fine of not more than five hundred dollars ($500) or
> **by** imprisonment in a county jail for not more than six months
> or **by** both such fine and imprisonment.

I have converted this excerpt from the California Penal Code into a postmodern poem. You are invited to read vertically as well as horizontally (e.g., **state, removed, owner, land**). You are invited to skip sections or, as with the **chorus,** to repeat sections set to your own music. You are invited, above all, to make a game out of self-important solemnity, just as the postmodern painter Marcel Duchamp did by painting a mustache on the Mona Lisa. In the process of thus desecrating the law, I have also made it much easier to understand. You can pick out the formulaic repetitions. You can see, gulp!, that the whole enchilada is a single sentence, and what the subject and verb ("Every person shall be punished!") really are.

THE OFFICIAL STYLE SUMMARIZED

Let's run over the basic elements of The Official Style again.

1. It is built on nouns, vague, general nouns. These nouns are often of Latin derivation, "shun" words like fixa*tion*, func*tion*, construc*tion*, educa*tion*, organiza*tion*, op*tion*, implementa*tion*, or other perennial favorites like flexibility, capability, concept, and so on.
2. These nouns are often, as in Broughton's game, modified by adjectives made up from other nouns like them, as in "incremental throughput" or "functional input."
3. All action is passive and impersonal. No active verbs and no direct objects. Never "I decided to fire him"

but "It has been determined that the individual's continued presence in the present personnel configuration would tend to be to the detriment of the ongoing operational efficiency of the organizational unit in which the individual is currently employed."

4. Nothing is called by its ordinary name. You don't decide to bomb a town; instead, "It has been determined to maintain an aggressive and operational attack posture." You don't set up an office, you "initiate an ongoing administrative facility."

5. The status quo is preserved in syntax. All motion is converted into stasis. The Official Style denies, as much as possible, the reality of action. You don't dislike someone, you "maintain a posture of disapproval toward" him. You don't decide to hire someone, you "initiate the hiring process." You add all necessary qualifications by stringing together prepositional phrases rather than by careful word choice or use of the possessive case. Above all, you make the simple sound complex, as in the following prizewinner.

AN OFFICIAL STYLE OSCAR

Official Style	*Plain English*
The purpose of this project is to develop the capability for institutions of higher learning and community agencies and organizations to coalesce for the development of community services that would maximize the available resources from a number of institutions and provide communication between priority needs and the responses of the educational needs of a given community.	This project aims to teach universities and community organizations how to work more efficiently together.

You can see the problem here. The plain English sounds *too simple*. A worthy project, no doubt, but who would ever fund anything as obvious as that?

We have, then, two weapons to combat The Official Style, not just one. We can *revise* it, as we have been doing in earlier chapters. Or, we can *play games with it*, as we have been doing here. We can banquet off the stuffiness of the prose itself. For, though it doesn't know it, and would deny it if charged, The Official Style aspires not to clarity but to poetry—the poetry of bureaucracy—and we can analyze it as such, just as I have done here. Both PM translation and poetic analysis should help you translate into and out of The Official Style when needed.

Writing on an electronic screen, using typographical rearrangement and reemphasis, lets us deploy both weapons at once. We can puncture the pomposity while we clarify the meaning. It is to these revisionary powers of the electronic screen that we must now turn.

CHAPTER 5

ELECTRONIC
LITERACY

When you display written words on an electronic screen rather than imprint them on paper, reading itself changes radically; "electronic literacy" turns out to differ in fundamental ways from "print literacy." And electronic literacy increasingly dominates the workplace. Anyone working in present-day America confronts these radical changes in expressive medium, in "literacy," in reading and writing, every day. Even a practical, hands-on guide like *Revising Prose* must pause to reflect on these changes, for they have transformed how the written word lives and works in human life.

Changes close to home first. We have already noticed how word processors enhance prose revision. They make it much easier not only to get the words "down" (though "on screen" rather than "on paper"!) but to take them up and move them around. And the speed with which revision takes place means, often, that more revision can take place when writing—as we usually do—under a deadline. No need to go through those one-day retyping turnarounds for each revision. And electronic spelling and grammar checkers and the electronic thesaurus, by speeding up ordinary procedures, further encourage revision. Global searches can find prepositional-phrase strings and tell you if every main verb is *is*. Use global search-and-replace to put a double space and carriage return at the end of each sentence for a page or two and you'll get a pretty good idea of sentence-length variation. Word-counters make computing the Lard Factor much faster. And changes in layout and typography become a handy analytical tool to find one's way in The Official Style's pathless prose woods. Because the computer is a rule-based device, it lends itself to a rule-based revision method. All in all, prose paramedics have never had it so easy.

VISUALIZATION AND VOICING

But digital text has changed literacy more profoundly than these helpful easements suggest. Most important, the whole relationship between verbal and visual communication is changing. Images more and more both supplement and replace written information. For statistical presentation of all sorts, old-fashioned pie charts and bar graphs have given way to more imaginative and three-dimensional renderings. Even simple spreadsheet programs encourage the visualization of numeric data. And computer graphics now routinely model all kinds of complex dynamic processes in three dimensions and real time. We are so used to the convention of print—linear, regular left-to-right and top-to-bottom, black-and-white, constant font and type size—that we have forgotten how constraining it is. Black-and-white print is remarkable not only for its power to express conceptual thought but for all the powers it renounces in doing so. No pictures, no color, no perspective. Up to now these things have been just too expensive. No longer. On the electronic screen, you can do them all and a lot more. And as electronic memory gets ever cheaper, they have come within the reach not only of graphics designers but of everyday wordsmiths as well.

The constraints of conventionally printed prose are slowly dissolving. If we can use color, font size and shape, three-dimensional effects like drop-shadow and the like, then we will use them. If we can intersperse text and graphics with ease, we'll come to depend on the combination. All these changes, in their turn, are changing how we write and indeed how we think. It is no exaggeration to say that electronic textual information has now become three-dimensional. The black-and-white letters-only convention concentrates on abstract thought—the "meaning"—to the exclusion of everything else. Tonal colorations there will always be—they are what we usually call "style"—but in print they work always beneath the surface, implicit rather than explicit. Bringing them to the surface takes time and trouble. With the electronic word, however, these tonal colorations can be explicit rather than implicit. We will be able, literally, to "color" our communications with one another. And there will be no going back, no abjuration of this new realm of communication. If you can write "in color," and choose not to, that too will be a "communication," and usually one you will not want to make. So don't be fooled by that black-and-white screen. How often nowadays do you watch black-and-white TV? And what does it seem like when you do?

What do these changes imply for literacy in the workplace and the schools and colleges which prepare for it? Well, for a start, they dramatize a need I have been advocating all through this book, a need to use the visual imagination in reading, writing, and revising. More than ever, we must notice the shape of prose. Up to now, "graphics" people tended to work in one office and "word" people in another. No more. From now on, graphics will be fundamental to a writer's training. Words and images are now inextricably intertwined in our common expressive repertoire. The desktop-publishing revolution reinforces this change at every point. Typography and layout, a special field before, in electronic display become an expressive parameter for all writers. My students, to take one revealing example, now commonly choose a font for their papers to fit the course, teacher, or assignment. The classic creed of the typographer has always been that the written surface should be transparent—never noticed for itself, serving only the meaning shining through its lucid waters. That theory needs adjustment. We will be looking *at* the prose surface as much as looking *through* it. And that, of course, is what *Revising Prose* has always had in mind. Revision means exactly this oscillation between looking *at* and looking *through* a prose surface. The nature of electronic text leads more directly to this *at/through* oscillation than does print, and thus invites revision in a way fixed print does not.

I've also been arguing that prose—now uniformly read in silence—should be *voiced*, at least in the auditory imagination. The digitized word reinforces and empowers this recommendation as well. Since the last edition of this book, voice communication has become a reality in computer communication. We can now talk to the computer and it can talk back. It will not be long before voicing will be a routine dimension of the electronic word. We will move from voice to writing to image and back again in ways new to humankind. The Official Style pushes prose to its voiceless extreme. We have seen that over and over; *read it aloud* and The Official Style sounds silly, absurdly pompous, often simply pointless. Voice is now returning to writing in ways so fundamental as to recall an oral culture rather than a written one. *Voiceless* prose just won't work much longer.

MULTIMEDIA PROSE

Computer programs now exist to make this new mixture of word, image, and sound easier to pursue. The same digitized information, to begin with, can be expressed as either word, sound, or picture. I own a cheap but wonderful program

(Laurie Spiegel's *Music Mouse*) which allows me to make music by drawing patterns on my mouse pad. Another one (*Jam Session*) allows me to play along with a variety of music groups, according to definite but adjustable musical boundary conditions, by typing on my computer keyboard. Ordinary commercial programs like these form but the trickle-down residue of a fundamental information revolution; information from different parts of the human sensorium now shares a common digital code.

Plato dreamed of such a union, hoping to find the common center for all knowledge in mathematics. Ordinary marketplace training now embodies it. Interactive videodisc technology, a basic format for much business, government, and military training, mixes sight and sound, word and image, as part of its standard operating procedure. Computer-assisted design and manufacturing programs regularly employ three-dimensional visual modeling as a fundamental conceptual tool. An entire new field of scientific creativity, called appropriately enough visualization, has been built about computer modeling techniques. And, on a more trivial desktop level, we are all inundated by CD-ROMs full of clip art.

Electronic literacy, then, will differ markedly from print literacy. It will mix alphabetic information with information coming from image and sound. Workers at every level will communicate in a richer but more complex informational sensorium. Writing will mean something different, and writers who don't know, and feel, this will find themselves the clerks of a forgotten mood.

VOLATILE TEXT AND TEXTUAL AUTHORITY

Other fundamental changes come with the electronic word. Perhaps foremost, *authority* diffuses itself between writer and reader. Although we seldom think of it thus, the print medium is fundamentally authoritarian. "In print" means unchangeable. You can't quarrel with it. This penumbra of authority goes back a long way. The Renaissance humanists resurrected the authority of classical Greek and Latin culture by editing that culture's documents into fixed printed texts. The authoritative edition means the unchanging edition, text fixed forever, a lodestone of cultural authority. We still feel that way about print. It *fixes* things. Electronic text *unfixes* them. It is by nature changeable, antiauthoritarian. If we don't like what it says, we can change it, ornament it, revise it, erase it, mock it in letters indistinguishable from the original ones. No one, so far as I know, has studied the role of print, as a technology, in the history of managerial authority, but it must play a central one. All that technology-based managerial authority is now changing. Ask any teacher of a computer-lab course. She'll tell you about the big change—the teacher is no longer the *teacher*. The patterns of authority have shifted, become democratized. This democratization means that the electronic word will mean something very different from the printed one. Anyone interested in writing of any sort must understand this change.

It operates, for a start, upon the very role the writer adopts as a writer. When we write we inevitably adopt a social role of some sort. Trying to bring this presentation of self to self-consciousness has been one of our main tasks in this book. Surely all of us have noticed that the kind of self we adopt in computer communication, especially on-line and, to a lesser degree, in electronic mail, differs from our "print" self. For reasons I leave to the psychologists, computers have from their beginnings evoked the game and play ranges of human motivation far more strongly than print. The whole hacker personality that created the computer was suffused with the competitive game impulse, but equally with the "for-its-own-sake" impulse to do something just to see if it could be done. This hacker mentality seems inevitably to creep in whenever we put our fingers on the computer's home row: we hold language more lightly in our hands; our sense of humor stands closer;

we can't take things, or ourselves, so seriously. A good pre-disposition this turns out to be—returning from theory to home concerns—for avoiding The Official Style and its systematic pomposity. The "dignity of print" has a lot to answer for. Let's hope that the electronic word preserves the muse of comedy that has hovered around its creation. At all events, it is something to be alert to if you are writing and revising prose in an electronic world. It has created a new kind of communications decorum.

ALLEGORICAL ALPHABETS

This book is not the place to illustrate the changes in store for us. In the first place, no book can: the book is just what electronic text is transcending. In the second place, *Revising Prose* is a hands-on guide, not a theoretical discussion. But perhaps an example or two can sketch the revolution in typography which the personal computer is bringing about.

The printed book, as we have known it since Gutenberg, depends on print as essentially transparent and un-self-conscious. We do not notice it as print. The book may be well designed or ill, and we may register that. But the kind of type selected, the size and shape of the letters, the white space between and around them, does not form part of the meaning. Making all these selections, "specing type" as the editors call it, is an editing and production task, not an authorial affair.

All this is now changing. Typography can now be—and I think increasingly will become—allegorical, part of the meaning, an authorial not an editing function. This will allow us to *see* prose characteristics that formerly we could only talk about. We will be able to analyze and revise prose in new ways, using new mixtures of alphabet and icon. We can begin to see how this process might work by using the font and graphics capabilities available on any graphics monitor.

Here is the kind of sentence people in academic life read all the time:

_____

The integration of a set of common value patterns with the internalized need-disposition structure of the constituent personalities is the core phenomenon of the dynamics of social systems.

Huh? The usual shapeless shopping bag of general concepts held together by "is" and prepositional glue. Here are three diagrams of its structure, diagrams anyone can construct on a personal computer.

The integration
of a set
of common value patterns
with the internalized need-disposition structure
of the constituent personalities
is the core phenomenon
of the dynamics
of social systems.

The	**integration**	of a set
of	**common value patterns**	
with the	**internalized need-disposition structure**	
of the	**constituent personalities**	
is the	**core phenomenon**	
of the	**dynamics**	
of	**social systems**.	

The		**integration** of a set
of	**common value**	**patterns**
with the	**inter. need-disp.**	**structure**
of the	**constituent**	**personalities**
is the	**core**	**phenomenon**
of the		**dynamics**
of	**social**	**systems**.

In the first, I have done one of our usual vertical preposition charts, but with a little enhancement to render the pattern more graphic. The second chart tries to see what relationship the general terms bear to one another by listing them separately from the prepositions that glue them together in a string. The separate listing shows you immediately what is wrong; the concepts in the list bear no discernible relationship to one another. Nothing in the concepts themselves tells us how they might be related; the pressures for connection fall entirely on the prepositions. They cannot bear it. Their breakdown makes the passage so hard to read. And the qualification of the key terms by adjectives, which themselves represent key terms —"common value patterns," "internalized need-disposition structure," "constituent personalities"—makes things still worse. So I rearranged the sentence into the third chart, trying to set off the key words and indicate graphically the three basic levels that compose the sentence. The lack of any fundamental relationship, causal or otherwise, between the central words in the right-hand column shows up even more. You can, given the syntax of the sentence, rearrange the central terms several different ways and still make sense of a sort. Try it.

Charts like this provide a powerful analytical tool. You needn't sit there cudgeling your brains in paralytic silence. You can start trying to make sense of things right on the screen, using your eyes and hands to help you think. The need to "spec type" stimulates you to see how the sentence really fits together. And you can, by type selection, both display your analysis and demonstrate your attitude toward it.

Here is a simpler sentence altogether: "These ideas create a frame for the paragraph." A series of typographical manipulations shows the stages of perception that follow from applying rules 3 and 4 of the PM—finding the action and putting it in a single, simple verb.

These ideas create a frame for the paragraph.

These ideas create a frame for the paragraph.

These ideas frame the paragraph.

These ideas frame the paragraph.

I used an outline typeface, one that frames each letter, to echo the "framing" action of the sentence. This kind of punning comment is just one of many available when type selection can be an authorial rather than an editorial function. In the next example, I changed type to show just where, in mid-sentence, the reader gets lost. The second type selection tries to depict this confusion visually.

Ordinary Typography

However, consciousness does exist and it stimulates an antagonistic relationship between the acceptance of the role of self-consciousness and the disregard of the knowledge which is indigenous to consciousness for the adaptation of a more sentimental role.

Allegorical Typography

However, consciousness does exist and it stimulates an antagonistic relationship between the acceptance of the role of self-consciousness and the disregard of the knowledge which is indigenous to consciousness for the adaptation of a more sentimental role.

You can use a similar technique to spotlight a persistent sound-clash pattern, here a hissing "s," "sh," and "t" in the prose of a biologist whose prose remains persistently tone deaf:

Since Darwin initially provided the means of testing for the existence of an evolutionary process and for its significance in accounting for the attributes of living organisms, biologists have accepted with increasing decisiveness the hypothesis that all attributes of life are outcomes of that simple process.

In the next example, also written by a professor, I've tried to portray graphically the shapeless, unfocused prose by printing the passage three times, in typefaces that become progressively easier to read. The first makes us look at the shape of

the sentence only, since it is so hard to read the typeface. We
have to look *at* rather than *through*. The second is easier, the
third easier still. It yields, in turn, to our usual graph of
the shopping-bag sentence; there I've tried to satirize the
wallboard monotony by making the prepositions huge and,
with a glance at the medieval subject of the passage, in a
"medieval" type.

It is one of the paradoxes of the history of rhetoric that what was in
Antiquity essentially an oral discipline for the pleading of law cases
should have become in the Middle Ages in one of its major aspects,
a written discipline for the drawing up of quasi-legal documents.

*It is one of the paradoxes of the history of rhetoric that what
was in Antiquity essentially an oral discipline for the pleading
of law cases should have become in the Middle Ages in one of
its major aspects, a written discipline for the drawing up of
quasi-legal documents.*

It is one of the paradoxes of the history of rhetoric that what
was in Antiquity essentially an oral discipline for the pleading of law cases should have become in the Middle Ages in
one of its major aspects, a written discipline for the drawing
up of quasi-legal documents.

It *is* one

of the paradoxes
of the history
of rhetoric that what **was**
in antiquity essentially an oral discipline
for the pleading of law cases should have become
in the Middle Ages
in one
of its major aspects, a written discipline
for the drawing up
of quasi-legal documents.

I've asked students repeatedly how they read large stretches of Official Style academic prose; the uniform answer has been "I skip from key term to key term and try to guess at their connection." I've tried to depict this habit in the next sentence:

> The idea of **action language implies** as the correct approach to the emotions **foregoing** the use of **substantives** in making **emotion-statements** and **employing** for this purpose only **verbs and adverbs** or adverbial locutions.

We might call this "highlighter reading"; it can provide a handy guide for revision. It may someday find its way into the printing conventions for wallboard prose like this, as a kind of running internal summary. Probably, though, it would prove too satirical.

In the following typographical rendering, I've tried to depict visually a sentence slowly running out of gas as it passes through its prepositional-phrase string. I've used italics at the end to emphasize how the central concept in the sentence has been placed in the least emphatic place possible, just before the sentence peters out completely.

Dr. Heartfelt has earned a reputation for excellence for the sharing of the wisdom of the path of *compassionate service* in the natural healing arts.

Diagramming prose rhythm in a printed book never works very well; it goes against the grain of the medium. I was trying, in the following chart, to visualize a sentence whose first half was metronomically monotonous but whose second half fell into a very rhythmical, indeed even symmetrical pattern. I also thought it might show how a change in typeface can sometimes indicate a quotation more forcefully than quotation marks.

While the whole world	even Roosevelt
felt a sense	of relief
at the escape	from war
at the time	of Munich

Churchill stood up in the House of Commons and
disregarding a storm of protest
somberly declared

We have sustained a total and unmitigated
defeat.

A final example springs from pure play. I had picked out a sentence from a student paper—"Etching will always be my love"—because it sounded silly to me. Should it be "I will always love etching"? Not much better. I wondered what typographical enhancement might do to it:

Etching will always be my love.

Etching will always be my love.

Etching will always be my love.

Etching will always be my love.

No luck. It just seems to get sillier and sillier. Can you figure out why?

THE ELECTRONIC WORD

I've presented these typographical transformations as tools of analysis, but they are tools of creation as well, and no doubt will be used as such when computer composition becomes commonplace. (How about the sound pattern in the last four words of the sentence I have just written? I would normally have revised it, but I'll let it stand.) The electronic word will mix creation and criticism, writing and revision, finally reading and writing themselves, which will alternate constantly in an interactive medium. Interactive computer fiction—detective games and the like—are doing this already. The whole idea of a fixed text, the center of the Western literary canon (at least since the Renaissance), now stands under attack. And our conception of the book—fixed, not interactive, linear, black-and-white—seems due for transformation as well. I have no idea where this cornucopia of changes will fetch us up, but clearly prose, and prose revision, will never be the same. Revising the electronic word will be easier, more challenging, creative, and much more fun. The kind of typographical manipulation and commentary we've been toying with provides just a hint of the coming metamorphosis of the word. With it will come a new understanding of prose style and, indeed, a new definition of prose itself.

I don't want to extend further this argument about the expressive opportunities created by computer display; as I said earlier, *Revising Prose* is not a theoretical book. But as much as I have said must, I think, be said in any book about prose revision. The electronic word has changed the whole matrix of written expression, just as digitization has transformed the marketplace itself. To ignore this state-change at the one level is as perilous as to ignore it at the other.

Let me end these brief but needful reflections with one that emerges from our labors at prose revision. The logic of a society built on information instead of, or in addition to, goods will lead us to a self-consciousness about words and the signals they broadcast far greater than now customary. The kind of verbal self-consciousness that now seems restricted to writers and literary critics will, by the very technological "logic" of an electronic information society, become a central professional skill. That new conception of prose—as wide as language itself, and as bright and sparkling and changeable as the electronic word can make it—offers a new and lively path whose ending none of us can foresee.

CHAPTER 6

WHY BOTHER?

I've been arguing that much of the prose problem in America comes from the cluster of goals and attributes that make up The Official Style. Inasmuch as this is true, the paramedic analogy holds and the prose can be revised using simple procedures. We have seen what The Official Style looks like: dominantly a noun style; a concept style; a style whose sentences have no artful design, no rhythm, or emphasis; an unreadable, voiceless, impersonal style; a style built on euphemism and various kinds of poetic diction; a style with a formulaic sentence structure, "is" plus a string of prepositional phrases before and after. And we've seen how to revise it. A set of do-it-yourself techniques, the Paramedic Method, handles the problem nicely.

TWO ANSWERS

But you may well be asking, at this point, "Why bother?" Why try to see in a blind world? There are two answers, or rather two kinds of answers. The first kind: "If you can see and others can't, you'll get ahead." Sometimes this is true and sometimes not. Generally, it helps if you write better prose. It makes for a better statement of purpose when you apply for law school or a job; later on, it will help you write a better legal brief or progress report or memo. But where The Official Style is mandated by rule or custom (as in some bureaucratic situations it is), plain prose may sound simpleminded or even flip. The sensible procedure here: learn both languages, the plain and The Official Style. Here, as always in the two millennia of rhetoric's history, there are rules that work, but there are no rules about when to apply those rules. I cannot better the answer that the likes of Aristotle, Cicero, and Quintilian have always returned. Learn the rules and then, through experience, train your intuition to apply them effectively. *Stylistic* judgment is, last as well as first, always *political* judgment. There is no dodging that ineluctable equation.

The second kind of answer is both simpler than the first and more complex. We've looked at many examples of inept writing—writing that ranges from shapeless to mindless. The second kind of answer to "Why bother?" is simply, "Are you willing to sign your name to what you have written? To present yourself in public—whether it matters to anyone else or not—as this kind of person?" In a sense, it is a simple question: "Whatever the advantage—or disadvantage—ought I do this?" The primary kind of moral question: If everyone else is committing murder, ought I do the same? Do you choose to encounter the world on its terms or on your own? A simple question but one we must all answer for ourselves. "The style is the man," people often say. Perhaps they mean that to this basic moral question you'll give the same answer for writing as for the rest of your behavior. Yet the question is complex, too, for what kind of behavior is "prose behavior"? Prose is usually described in a moral vocabulary—"sincere," "open" or "devious," and "hypocritical"—but is this vocabulary justified? Why, for that matter, has it been so moralistic? Why do so many people feel that bad prose threatens the foundations of civilization? And why, in fact, do we think "bad" the right word to use for it?

STYLE AND SELF

Let's start with the primary ground for morality, the self. We may think of the self as both a dynamic and a static entity. It is static when we think of ourselves as having central, fixed selves independent of our surroundings, an "I" we can remove from society without damage, a central self inside our heads. But it becomes dynamic when we think of ourselves as actors playing social roles, a series of roles that vary with the social situation in which we find ourselves. Such a social self amounts to the sum of all the public roles we play. Our complex identity comes from the constant interplay of these two kinds of self. Our final "self" is usually a mixed one, few of us being completely the same in all situations or, conversely, social chameleons who change with every context. The self grows and develops through the free interplay between these two kinds of self. If we were completely sincere we would always say exactly what we think—and cause social chaos. If we were always acting an appropriate role, we would be certifiably insane. Reality, for each of us, presents itself as constant oscillation between these two extremes.

When we say that writing is sincere, we mean that somehow it has managed to express this complex oscillation, this complex self. It has caught the accent of a particular self, a particular mixture of the two selves. Sincerity can't point to any specific verbal configuration, of course, since sincerity varies as widely as human beings themselves. The sincere writer has not said exactly how she felt in the first words that occurred to her. That might produce a revolutionary tirade, or "like you know" conversational babble, or the gross mistakes we've been reviewing. Nor has a sincere writer simply borrowed a fixed language, as when a bureaucrat writes in The Official Style. She has managed to create a style which, like the social self, can become part of society, can work harmoniously in society and, at the same time, like the central self, can represent her unique selfhood. She holds her two selves in balance; this is what "authority" in prose really means.

Now reverse this process. Writing prose involves for the writer an integration of self, a deliberate act of balancing its two component parts. It represents an act of socialization, and it is by repeated acts of such socialization that we become sociable beings, that we grow up. Thus the act of writing models the presentation of self in society; prose reality rehearses us for social reality. It is not a question of a preexistent self making its message known to a preexistent society. It is not, initially, a question of message at all. Writing clarifies, strengthens, and energizes the self, renders individuality rich, full, and social. This does not mean writing that flows, as Terry Southern immortally put it, "right out of the old guts onto the goddamn paper." Just the opposite. Only by taking the position of the reader toward one's own prose, putting a reader's pressure on it, can the self be made to grow into full sociability. Writing should enhance and expand the self, allow it to try out new possibilities, tentative selves.

The moral ingredient in writing, then, works first not on the morality of the message but on the nature of the sender, on the complexity of the self. "Why bother?" To invigorate and enrich your selfhood, to increase, in the most literal sense, your self-consciousness. Writing, properly pursued, does not make you better. It makes you more alive. This is why our growing illiteracy ought to distress us. It tells us something, something alarming, about the impoverishment of our selves. We say that we fear written communication will break down. Unlikely. And if it does we can always do what we do anyway— pick up the phone. Something more fundamental stands at stake, the selfhood and sociability of the communicators. We are back to the basic peculiarity of writing: it is premeditated utterance, and in that premeditation lives its first if not its only value. "Why bother?" "To find out who I really am." It is not only what we *think* that we discover in writing, but what we *are* and *can construct ourselves to be*.

We can now see why the purely neutral, transparent style is so hard to write and so rare, and why we take to jargon, to The Official Style, to all the varieties of poetic diction, verbal ornament, with such alacrity. We are doing more in writing, any writing, than transmitting neutral messages. We want to convey our feelings about what we say, our attitude toward the human relationships we are thus establishing. Neutral communications do not come naturally to people. What matters most to us is our relationships with our fellow creatures. These urges continually express themselves through what we write. They energize what we call style. Style has attracted a moralistic vocabulary because it expresses all the patterns of human behavior that morality must control. This moralistic vocabulary leads to considerable confusion, but it arises naturally enough from the way human beings use literary style.

How rare a purely neutral human relationship really is you can see simply by reflecting on your daily life. Is there any response, however trivial, that we don't color with hand gestures, facial expressions, postures of the body? Human beings are nonstop expressers, often through minute subconscious clues. We sense, immediately, that a friend is angry at us by the way he says "Hello." He doesn't say "Go to hell, you skunk" instead of "Hello." He doesn't need to. Tense vocal chords, pursed lips, a curt bob of the head perhaps, do just as well. No one has put a percentage figure to this kind of human communication, but it far outranks plain statement in frequency and importance. The same truth prevails for written communication. We are always trying to say more than we actually do. This stylistic voice-over technique is our natural way of speaking.

VALUE JUDGMENTS

We can now begin to see what kinds of value judgments make sense about prose and what kinds don't. The prevailing wisdom teaches that the best prose style is the most transparent, the least seen; prose ideally aspires to a perfect neutrality; like the perfect secretary, it gets the job done without intruding. Such ideal prose rarely occurs. Might that be because it really isn't ideal? Doesn't ideal neutrality rule out most of what we call good prose? The ideal document of perfect neutrality would be a grocery list. (And think of how we immediately flood that neutral document with likes and dislikes, with *emotions* — not sardines *again*!) We mean by "good prose" something different from impersonal transparency. We mean a style suffused with a sense of human relationships, of specific occasions and why they matter. We mean a style that expresses a genuinely complex and fully socialized self.

We've cleared up a lot of muddy writing in this book. The metaphor "clear up" is clear enough, and there is no reason not to use it, but we can now explain more precisely what we have been doing. An incoherent style is "clear enough." It depicts clearly an incoherent mind, an incoherent person. Looked at in this way, all prose is clear. Revision aims to "clear up" the *person*, to present a self more coherent, more in control. A mind thinking, not a mind asleep. It aims, that is, not to denature the human relationship that prose sets up but to enhance and enrich it. It tries not to squeeze out the expression of personality but to make such expression possible, not to squeeze out all record of a particular occasion and its human relationships but to make them maximally clear. Again, this is why we worry so much about bad prose. It signifies incoherent people, failed social relationships. This worry makes sense only if we feel that prose, ideally, should express human relationships and feelings, not abolish them.

Think, for example, about a familiar piece of prose we might all call successful, Lincoln's *Gettysburg Address*. Its brevity has been much praised, but the brevity does not work in a vacuum. It makes sense, becomes expressive, only in relation to the occasion. Lincoln took for his subject the inevitable gap between words and deeds. At Gettysburg, this gap was enormous, and the shortness of Lincoln's speech does reverence to it. No speech could do justice to what had happened at

Gettysburg. Lincoln's brevity did not remove the emotion of the occasion but intensified it; it did not ignore the occasion's human relationships but celebrated them. We think it a monument to brevity and clarity not because it neutralizes human emotion but because it so superbly enshrines just the emotions that fit the occasion.

"Vascular Disturbances" vs. Bleeding from the Ears

We might, as a contrasting example, consider a modern instance of public prose. In 1977, the Federal Aviation Administration published a document called *Draft Environmental Impact Statement for the Proposed Public Acquisition of the Existing Hollywood-Burbank Airport.* It discussed, in two volumes and about fifteen hundred pages, the noise and pollution problems the airport caused and what might happen if the Lockheed Corporation sold it to a consortium of interested city governments. The statement also included extensive testimony about the airport by private citizens. The statement itself provides a perfect—if at times incomprehensible—example of The Official Style; the citizens, with some exceptions, speak and write plain English. The statement as a whole thus constitutes an invaluable extended example of how the two styles conflict in real life.

The issue posed was simple. Lockheed was going to shut the airport down and sell the land if the city governments didn't buy it. Would the loss of airport jobs and public transportation be compensated by the increased peace and quiet in the East San Fernando Valley? Horrible noise on the one hand; money on the other. How do you relate them to one another? The different styles in the statement put the problem in different ways. They seem, sometimes, to be describing different problems. Here's a sample of the statement's archetypal Official Style:

101

The findings of ongoing research have shown that a number of physiological effects occur under conditions of noise exposure. . . . These studies demonstrate that noise exposure does influence bodily changes, such as the so-called vegetative functions, by inhibition of gastric juices, lowered skin resistance, modified pulse rate and increased metabolism. . . .

Other studies have investigated the generalized physiological effects of noise in relation to cardiovascular disturbances, gastrointestinal problems, impairment of performance on motor tracking tasks and vascular disturbances, as well as various physical ailments. Miller (1974) states that, "Steady noise of 90 dB increases tension in all muscles." Welch (1972) concludes that "environmental sound has all-pervasive effects on the body, influencing virtually every organ system and function that has been studied," and Cohen (1971) summarized that "the distressing effects of noise alone or combined with other stress factors can eventually overwhelm man's capability for healthy adjustment with resultant physical or mental ailments. . . ."

The VTN survey determined the presence of annoyance reactions which have been identified as indicators of stressful response to environmental noise among respondents both inside and outside the noise impact area. As is reported in Section 2.5.3 (Annoyance Reactions as Determinants of Community Response to Airport Noise) of this chapter, individuals' beliefs about the noise and the noise source tend to determine their reactions to its occurrence and the amount of disturbance it creates. . . .

When asked for the three things they liked least about their neighborhood, 14.2 percent of the respondents in the high noise exposure area, compared to only 5.3 percent of those residing in the low noise exposure area, indicated aircraft noise among the three. It appears from these observations that Hollywood-Burbank Airport does produce annoyance reactions among residents of the East Valley, which indicates a perception of environmental stress associated with Airport noise.

No need to do a detailed analysis at this stage of the game — the formula as before. In this distanced and impersonal world, no one ever suffers; they experience "the presence of annoyance reactions." And, in the report's ever-cautious style, it only "appears" that the airport produces such reactions among residents. Later, in the residents' comments, that "appearance" becomes an oppressive reality.

Human beings, we need to remind ourselves here, are social beings. Our reality is a social reality. Our identity draws its felt life from our relation to other people. We become uneasy if, for extended periods of time, we neither hear nor see other people. We feel uneasy with The Official Style for the same reason. It has no human voice, no face, no personality behind it. It creates no society, encourages no social conversation. We feel that it is unreal. The "better" it is, the more typical, the more unreal it becomes. And so we can answer the question of whether you can write a "good" Official Style. Yes, of course, when you must work in The Official Style, you can try to observe its conventions in a minimal way. But the closer you get to the impersonal essence of The Official Style, the more distant any felt human reality becomes.

But public prose need not erase human reality. It can do just the opposite, as in the following passage from the same report—a letter from a homeowners' group president. With it, we return to human life.

Our Homeowners Association was formed about a year and a half ago principally because of an overwhelming fear of what might happen to our homes, schools and community as a result of any steps which might be taken by Lockheed and/or the City of Burbank. Our community is inexorably linked to Hollywood-Burbank Airport. The northern part of the North/South runway is in our city. . . .

Our community consists of a vast majority of single-family residences, and long-time owners with "paid in full" or "almost paid up" mortgages. We have been told, "You moved in next to the airport, it was there before you were." This is true in most cases. But, and this is a big "but"—it was an entirely different airport when most of us moved into the area. Twenty to

25 years ago, the airport was "home" to small planes. We actually enjoyed watching them buzz around, and many of us spent Sunday afternoons at the airport while our children were amused watching the little planes. However, the advent of the jet plane at HBA changed the entire picture. Suddenly we were the neighbors of a Noise Factory! . . .

Our children are bombarded with noise in 2 local elementary schools, Roscoe and Glenwood. Teachers have to stop teaching until the noise passes over and everyone waits "for the next one." If the school audiometrist wants an in-depth test for a child with questionable hearing, the child must be taken away from the school altogether to eliminate outside noises.

Our backyards, streets, parks and churches, too, are inundated with noise. . . . Noise is an ever-constant fact of life for us. There is seldom a time when one cannot hear a plane somewhere in the vicinity—it may be "up" or it may be "down," but once a motor is turned on, we hear it!

We might well be asked, "Why do you continue to live in such a place?" Put in plain and simple terms—we have no place else to go! Years have passed and we have put more money into our mortgages and into our property. We have developed long-time friendships with neighbors and the Community. We don't want to move! . . .

Where do we go? Who is going to pay us—and how much will we be paid—for being uprooted? Who sets the price on losing a street and an entire neighborhood full of long-time friends? If 7 schools are to be closed, where do the children go? What happens to the faculty and staff at the schools? The parochial schools? The small business man who sells consumer goods—what happens when there is no one to sell to?

A living voice! Human society! Plain English, in such a context, takes on the moral grandeur of epic, of the high style. The language of ordinary life reasserts our common humanity. Precisely the humanity, we have now come to see, The Official Style seeks to banish. It is a bad style, then, because it denatures human relations. When we consider that it is becoming the accepted language for the organizations that govern our human relations, we can begin to see how stylistic and moral issues converge.

Our current literacy crisis may come, then, from more than inattention, laziness, or even the diabolical purposes of The Official Style. It may come, ultimately, from our meager ideal for prose. We say that what we want is only a serviceable tool—useful, neutral, durable, honest, practical, and so on. But none of us takes such an attitude even toward our tools! If we earn our living with them, we love them. We clean and polish and lubricate them. We prefer one kind to another for quirky, personal reasons. We modify them. We want them not only to do a job but to express us, the attitude we take toward our job. So, too, with prose. We hunger for ceremony, for attitude, for ornament. It is no accident that bureaucrats play games with buzz words, build what amounts to purely ornamental patterns, create a *poetic* diction. These games express an attitude, albeit an ironically despairing one, toward what they are doing, the spirit in which they work. Jargons are created, too, for the same reason, to express a mystique, the spirit in which work is done. And, like a student's incoherence, they have their own eloquence, reflect clearly a habit of thought, a way of doing business. When we object to the prose, we are really objecting to the habit of thought, the bureaucratic way of life. It is because, paradoxically enough, the style is so clear, so successfully communicates a style of life, that we so feel its emotional impoverishment.

"No Profit Is Where Is No Pleasure Taken"

We have two choices, then, in regard to prose. We can allow the expression of personality and social relationships and try to control them, or we can ban them and try to extinguish them. Perhaps we should try the first alternative for a while.

We've tried the second for the better part of a century and we know where it leads. It leads to where we are now, to The Official Style. For those of us working alone to improve our prose, the choice is even clearer. Even if society disregards the importance of words, we must go in the other direction, train ourselves to notice them and to notice them as much as "content." A style that at first seems peculiar may not be a "bad" style but simply eloquent about an unexpected kind of reality, one that you may or may not like. Try to keep clear in your mind when you are responding to the words and when to the situation they represent. You'll find that you do first the one and then the other. You'll be rehearsing the same kind of oscillation we have already found to be at the base of stylistic revision. You'll have trained your pattern of attention in just the same way that an artist trains her eyes or a musician his ears. After all, you can't revise what you can't see. Only by learning to see the styles around you can you go beyond a fixed set of rules, a paramedic procedure.

In fact, in the long run, that is what any fixed set of rules ideally ought to do. It ought to guide us in training our verbal vision, expanding our intuition about words. Rules, analytic devices, are a shortcut to vision but no real substitute for being able to *see* a prose pattern. The paramedic analogy here breaks down. Beyond paramedicine lies medicine; beyond the specific analysis of specific style—what we have been doing here—lies the study of style in general. Verbal style can no more be fully explained by a set of rules, stylistic or moral, than can any other kind of human behavior. Intuition, trained intuition, figures as strongly in the one as in the other. You must learn how to see, and that learning is not entirely a rule-based proceeding.

Prose style, then, does not finally come down to a set of simple rules about clarity, brevity, and sincerity. It is as complicated as the rest of human behavior, and this because it forms part of that behavior as well as expressing it. People who tell you that mastering prose style is simple are kidding you. They make reading and writing grotesquely simplistic, in fact unreal. As students, all of us often complained about the "unreality" of our school life, but just where school life at any level is *most real*—in the central act of verbal expression— we most yearned for simplification. Well, none of us can have it both ways. You can choose the moralizing, rule-centered world, with its simplistic static conception of self and society, but you must not be surprised, when you try to use it in the real world, if it seems "unreal" in theory and backfires in practice. The other road is harder. You have to read and write and pay attention to both. If you do, you'll begin to see with what finesse we humans can communicate the subtleties of behavior. You'll begin, for the first time, to become self-conscious about the language you speak and hence about the society you live in. You will become more alive. And you'll begin to suspect what is perhaps a third answer to the question, "Why bother?" Because it's much more fun than writing The Official Style for the rest of your life. Shakespeare had it right: "No profit is where is no pleasure taken."

TERMS

You can see things you don't know the names for, but in prose style, as in everything else, it is easier to see what you know how to describe. The psychological ease that comes from calling things by their proper names has not often been thought a useful goal by modern pedagogy. As a result, inexperienced writers often find themselves reduced to talking about "smoothness," "flow," and other meaningless generalities when they are confronted by a text. And so here are some basic terms.

PARTS OF SPEECH

In traditional English grammar, there are eight parts of speech: verbs, nouns, pronouns, adjectives, adverbs, prepositions, conjunctions, and interjections. *Grammar*, in its most general sense, refers to all the rules that govern how meaningful statements can be made in any language. *Syntax* refers to sentence structure, to word order. *Diction* means simply word choice. *Usage* means linguistic custom.

Verbs

1. Verbs have two voices, active and passive.
An *active verb* indicates the subject acting:
Jack *kicks* Bill.
A *passive verb* indicates the subject acted upon:
Bill *is kicked by* Jim.
2. Verbs come in three moods: indicative, subjunctive, and imperative.
A verb in the *indicative mood* says that something is a fact. If it asks a question, it is a question about a fact:
Jim kicks Bill. Has Bill kicked Jim yet?
A verb in the *subjunctive mood* says that something is a wish, hypothetical, or contrary to fact, rather than a fact:
If Jim *were* clever, he would kick Bill.
A verb in the *imperative mood* issues a command:
Jim, *kick* Bill.
3. A verb can be either transitive or intransitive.
A *transitive verb* takes a direct object:
Jim *kicks* Bill.
An *intransitive verb* does not take a direct object. It represents action without a specific goal:
Lori *runs* every day.
The verb "to be" ("is," "was," and so on) is often called a *linking verb* because it links subject and predicate without expressing a specific action:
Elaine *is* a movie mogul.
4. English verbs have six tenses: present, past, present perfect, past perfect, future, and future perfect.
Present: Jim *kicks* Bill.
Past: Jim *kicked* Bill.

Present perfect: Jim *has kicked* Bill.
Past perfect: Jim *had kicked* Bill.
Future: Jim *will kick* Bill.
Future perfect: Jim *will have kicked* Bill.
The present perfect, past perfect, and future perfect are called compound tenses. Each tense can have a progressive form. (e.g., Present progressive: Jim *is kicking* Bill.)

5. Verbs in English have three so-called infinitive forms: *infinitive, participle,* and *gerund.* These verb forms often function as adjectives or nouns.
   Infinitive:
   To assist Elaine isn't easy.
   (When a word separates the "to" in an infinitive from its complementary form, as in "to directly stimulate" instead of "to stimulate," the infinitive is said to be a *split infinitive.* Most people think this separation is something we should avoid if possible.)
   Participles and gerunds have the same form; when the form is used as an adjective, it is called a *participle,* when used as a noun, a *gerund.*
   Participles:
   Present participle:
   Elaine was in an *arguing* mood.
   Past participle:
   Lori's presentation was very well *argued.*
   Gerund:
   Arguing with Elaine is no fun.
   Verbs that take "it" or "there" as subjects are said to be in an *impersonal construction*: "It has been decided to fire him" or "There has been a personnel readjustment."

Nouns

A noun names something or somebody. A proper noun names a particular being or place—Elaine, Pittsburgh.

1. *Number.* The singular number refers to one ("a cat"), plural to more than one ("five cats").
2. *Collective nouns.* Groups may be thought of as a single unit, as in "the army," and thus take a singular verb.

Pronouns

A *pronoun* is a word used instead of a noun. There are different kinds:

1. *Personal pronouns*: I, me, him . . .
2. *Intensive pronouns*: myself, yourself . . .
3. *Relative pronouns*: who, which, that. These must have antecedents, words they refer back to. "Lori has a talent (antecedent) that (relative pronoun) Elaine does not possess."
4. *Indefinite pronouns*: somebody, anybody, anything
5. *Interrogative pronouns*: who? what?

Adjectives

An *adjective* modifies a noun: "Lori was a *good* hiker."

Adverbs

An *adverb* modifies a verb: "Lori hiked *swiftly* up the trail."

Prepositions

A *preposition* connects a noun or pronoun with a verb, an adjective, or another pronoun: "I ran *into* her arms" or "The girl *with* the blue scarf."

Conjunctions

Conjunctions join sentences or parts of them. There are two kinds, coordinating and subordinating.

1. *Coordinating conjunctions*—and, but, or—connect statements of equal status: "Bill ran *and* Jim fell" or "I got up *but* soon fell down."
2. *Subordinating conjunctions*—that, when, because—connect a main clause with a subordinate one: "I thought *that* they had left."

Interjections

A sudden outcry: *"Wow!"*

Possessives

Singular: A *worker's* hat. Plural: The *workers'* hats. ("It's," however, equals "it is." **The possessive is "its"—no apostrophe!**)

SENTENCES

Every sentence must have both a subject and a verb, stated or implied: "Elaine (subject) directs (verb)."

Three Kinds

1. A *declarative sentence* states a fact: "Elaine directs films."
2. An *interrogative sentence* asks a question: "Does Elaine direct films?"
3. An *exclamatory sentence* registers an exclamation: "Does she ever!"

Three Basic Structures

1. A *simple sentence* makes one self-standing assertion, that is, has one main clause: "Elaine directs films."
2. A *compound sentence* makes two or more self-standing assertions, that is, has two main clauses: "Elaine directs

films and Lori is a tax lawyer" or "Jim kicks Bill and Bill feels it and Bill kicks Jim back."

3. A *complex sentence* makes one self-standing assertion and one or more dependent assertions in the form of subordinate clauses dependent on the main clause: "Elaine, who has just finished directing *Jim Kicks Bill*, must now consult Lori about her tax problems before she can start blocking out *Being Kicked: The Sequel*."

In *compound sentences*, the clauses are connected by *coordinating conjunctions*; in *complex sentences*, by *subordinating conjunctions*.

Restrictive and Nonrestrictive Relative Clauses

A *restrictive clause* modifies directly, and so restricts the meaning of the antecedent it refers back to: "This is the tire *that blew out on the freeway*." One specific tire is referred to. In such clauses the relative clause is not set off by a comma.

A *nonrestrictive clause*, though still a dependent clause, does not directly modify its antecedent and is set off by commas. "These tires, *which are quite expensive*, never blow out on the freeway."

Appositives

An *appositive* is an amplifying word or phrase placed next to the term it refers to and set off by commas: "Henry VIII, *a glutton for punishment*, rode out hunting even when sick and in pain."

BASIC SENTENCE PATTERNS

What words do you use to describe the basic syntactic patterns in a sentence? In addition to the basic types, declarative, interrogative, and exclamatory, and the basic forms of simple, compound, and complex, other terms sometimes come in handy.

Parataxis and Hypotaxis

Parataxis: Phrases or clauses arranged independently, in a coordinate construction, and often without connectives (e.g., "I came, I saw, I conquered").

Hypotaxis: Phrases or clauses arranged in a dependent subordinate relationship (e.g., "I came, and after I came and looked around a bit, I decided, well, why not, and so conquered").

The adjectival forms are *paratactic* and *hypotactic* (e.g., "Hemingway favors a paratactic syntax while Faulkner prefers a hypotactic one").

Asyndeton and Polysyndeton

Asyndeton: Connectives are omitted between words, phrases, or clauses (e.g., "I've been stressed, distressed, beat down, beat up, held down, held up, conditioned, reconditioned").

Polysyndeton: Connectives are always supplied between words and phrases, or clauses, as when Milton talks about Satan pursuing his way, "And swims, or sinks, or wades, or creeps, or flies."

The adjectives are *asyndetic* and *polysyndetic*.

Periodic Sentence

A *periodic sentence* is a long sentence with a number of elements, usually balanced or antithetical, standing in a clear syntactical relationship to each other. Usually it suspends the conclusion of the sense until the end of the sentence, and so is sometimes said to use a *suspended syntax*. A perfect example is the passage from Lord Brougham's defense of Queen Caroline quoted in Chapter 3. A periodic sentence shows us a pattern of thought that has been fully worked out, whose power relationships of subordination have been carefully determined, and whose timing has been climactically ordered. In a periodic sentence, the mind has finished working on the thought, left it fully formed.

There is no equally satisfactory antithetical term for the opposite kind of sentence, a sentence whose elements are loosely related to one another, follow in no particularly antithetical climactic order, and do not suspend its grammatical completion until the close. Such a style is often called a *running style* or a *loose style*, but the terms remain pretty vague. The loose style, we can say, often reflects a mind *in the process of thinking* rather than, as in the periodic sentence, having already completely ordered its thinking. A sentence so loose as to verge on incoherence, grammatical or syntactical, is often called a *run-on sentence.*

Isocolon

The Greek word means, literally, syntactic units of equal length, and it is used in English to describe the repetition of phrases of equal length and corresponding structure. Preachers, for example, often depend on isocolon to build up a rhythmic pattern or develop a series of contrasting ideas. Falstaff parodies this habit in Shakespeare's *1 Henry IV*: "Well, God give *thee the spirit of persuasion* and *him the ears of profiting*, that *what thou speakest may move* and *what he hears may be believed*, that *the true prince* may, for recreation sake, prove *a false thief.*" And later in the play, "Harry, now I do *not* speak to thee *in drink but in tears, not in pleasure but in passion, not in words only, but in woes also.*"

Chiasmus

Chiasmus is the basic pattern of antithetical inversion, the AB : BA pattern. President John Kennedy used it in his inaugural address:

A	**B**
Ask not *what your country*	*can do for you*, but
B	**A**
what you can do	*for your country.*

Anaphora

When you begin a series of phrases, clauses, or sentences with the same word or phrase, you are using *anaphora*. So Shakespeare's Henry V to some henchpersons who have betrayed him:

> Show men dutiful?
> *Why, so didst thou.* Seem they grave and learned?
> *Why, so didst thou.* Come they of noble family?
> *Why, so didst thou.* Seem they religious?
> *Why, so didst thou.*
>
> (*Henry V*, II, ii.)

Tautology

Repetition of the same idea in different words. In many ways, The Official Style is founded on this pattern. Here's a neat example from Shakespeare:

> *Lepidus.* What manner o'thing is your crocodile?
> *Antony.* It is shap'd, sir, like itself, and it is as broad as it has breadth. It is just so high as it is, and moves with its own organs. It lives by that which nourisheth it, and the elements once out of it, it transmigrates.
> *Lepidus.* What colour is it of?
> *Antony.* Of its own colour too.
> *Lepidus.* 'Tis a strange serpent.
> *Antony.* 'Tis so. And the tears of it are wet.
>
> (*Antony and Cleopatra*, II, vii.)

NOUN STYLE AND VERB STYLE

Every sentence must have a noun and a verb, but one can be emphasized, sometimes almost to the exclusion of the other. The Official Style—strings of prepositional phrases + "is" —

exemplifies a noun style *par excellence*. Here are three examples, the first of a noun style, the second of a verb style, and the third of a balanced noun-verb mixture.

Noun Style

There is in turn a two-fold structure of this "binding-in." In the first place, by virtue of internalization of the standard, conformity with it tends to be of personal, expressive and/or instrumental significance to ego. In the second place, the structuring of the reactions of alter to ego's action as sanctions is a function of his conformity with the standard. Therefore conformity as a direct mode of the fulfillment of his own need-dispositions tends to coincide with the conformity as a condition of eliciting the favorable and avoiding the unfavorable reactions of others.

(Talcott Parsons, *The Social System* [Glencoe, Ill.: Free Press, 1951], p. 38.)

Verb Style

Patrols, sweeps, missions, search and destroy. It continued every day as if part of sunlight itself. I went to the colonel's briefings every day. He explained how effectively we were keeping the enemy off balance, not allowing them to move in, set up mortar sites, and gather for attack. He didn't seem to hate them. They were to him like pests or insects that had to be kept away. It seemed that one important purpose of patrols was just for them to take place, to happen, to exist; there had to be patrols. It gave the men something to do. Find the enemy, make contact, kill, be killed, and return. Trap, block, hold. In the first five days, I lost six corpsmen—two killed, four wounded.

(John A. Parrish, *12, 20 & 5: A Doctor's Year in Vietnam* [Baltimore: Penguin Books, 1973], p. 235.)

Mixed Noun-Verb Style

We know both too much and too little about Louis XIV ever to succeed in capturing the whole man. In externals, in the mere business of eating, drinking, and dressing, in the outward routine of what he loved to call the *métier du roi*, no historical character, not even Johnson or Pepys, is better known to us; we can even, with the aid of his own writings, penetrate a little of the majestic facade which is Le Grand Roi. But when we have done so, we see as in a glass darkly. Hence the extraordinary number and variety of judgments which have been passed upon him; to one school, he is incomparably the ablest ruler in modern European history; to another, a mediocre blunderer, pompous, led by the nose by a succession of generals and civil servants; whilst to a third, he is no great king, but still the finest actor of royalty the world has ever seen.

(W. H. Lewis, *The Splendid Century: Life in the France of Louis XIV* [New York: Anchor Books, 1953], p. 1.)

PATTERNS OF RHYTHM AND SOUND

Meter

The terms used for scanning (marking the meter of) poetry sometimes prove useful for prose as well.

iamb: unstressed syllable followed by a stressed one (e.g., in vólve).
trochee: opposite of iamb (e.g., ám ber).
anapest: two unstressed syllables and one stressed syllable (e.g., there he góes).
dactyl: opposite of anapest, one stressed syllable followed by two unstressed ones (e.g., óp er ate).

These patterns form *feet*. If a line contains two, it is a *dimeter*; three, a *trimeter*; four, a *tetrameter*; five, a *pentameter*; six, a *hexameter*. The adjectival forms are *iambic, trochaic, anapestic,* and *dactylic*.

119

Sound Resemblances

Alliteration: This originally meant the repetition of initial consonant sounds but came to mean repetition of consonant sounds wherever they occurred, and now is often used to indicate vowel-sound repetition (also called assonance) as well. You can use it as a general term for this kind of sound play: "Peter Piper picked a peck of pickled peppers"; "Bill will always swill his fill."

Homoioteleuton: This jawbreaker refers, in Latin, to words with similar endings, usually case endings. An English analogy would be "looked" and "booked." You can use it for cases like this, to describe, for example, the "shun" words—"function," "organization," "facilitation"—and the sound clashes they cause.

For further explanation of the basic terms of grammar, see George O. Curme's *English Grammar* in the Barnes & Noble College Outline Series. For a fuller discussion of rhetorical terms like *chiasmus* and *asyndeton*, see Richard A. Lanham's *A Handlist of Rhetorical Terms*, 2nd ed., University of California Press, 1991. For a fuller discussion of prose style, see Richard A. Lanham's *Analyzing Prose*, Macmillan/Scribner's, 1983.

INDEX